Open Before You Open Your Legs

What Ladies Should Consider Before
Intimately Engaging

BRITTNEY PRESSLEY

Open Your Mind Before You Open Your Legs
published by:
Brittney Pressley
Alexandria, VA

Edited by Tanya Davis
Cover Design by Mark Davis
Author Portrait photographed by Chynna Davis

ISBN: 978-0-9890345-2-4(sc)

ISBN: 978-0-9890345-4-8(ebook)

ALSO BY BRITTNEY PRESSLEY:

Loving Inward, Living Outward, Looking Forward

Personal Blog: mind-does-matter.blogspot.com

Registered Trademarks on pages 7, 18, 19, 30, 31, 34, 61, 62, 80, 81, 82, 86, 119, 139, 151, 155, 163

Printed in the USA by
Morris Publishing ®
3212 E. Hwy 30 • Kearney, NE 68847
800-650-7888 • www.morrispublishing.com

This book is dedicated

To Millie,
Hours and hours of conversation inspired the birth of this book. Thank you for sharing your wisdom and being open to answering thousands of my burning questions.

To Ron,
Thank you for schooling me and listening to all of my crazy stories. You are my 'Dating Therapist' –
thank you for never charging!

Acknowledgments

*Thank you to my favorite Editor and Graphic Designer;
let's keep this streak going! This is just the beginning.*

A special thanks to:

Merieta Bayati
Timothy Davis
Rachel DiNardi
Megan Harpe
Azaria Keeling
Curtis Rogers
Nicholas A. Rogers
Derron Tapp
Theo Wells IV

for your insightful contributions

Contents

Section IV: Just So You Know

Section V: When You're In A Serious Relationship

Foreword

By: Anonymous

For the longest time, I couldn't understand why I stayed in my marriage for so long. I thought I was happy – I thought I was in love. I knew that once you had kids it wasn't about you anymore. When you're married, you endure; or at least that's what I saw. I saw other women in my family stay in their marriages; they acted like nothing was wrong. I found myself doing the same exact thing although I didn't see it at the time. I didn't realize how much of an impact childhood and culture have on the way that we approach our relationships – that is until now.

Although dysfunction felt normal to me at the time I have since discovered (after many hours of painful self-reflection) that I am in control of what 'normal' means; and I have in fact redefined its meaning. What you don't know you can't change! If you want to move forward in life you have to first look at your past – what are all of the cultural norms that you thought were right; *that felt right*? Instead of having a checklist for the guy you are dating, have a checklist for yourself! If I can leave you with four main pieces of advice from what I have learned from my experiences with relationships, it would be:

A. **Get yourself together.** Love yourself enough to not accept certain things. Mental, physical, and verbal abuse is never okay. Don't confuse 'like' with love. Second chances don't always pan out – be cautious about who you are giving them to. Everyone you are surrounded by has an influence on your life, be it positively or negatively. Be clear on *who* you are and be comfortable with the direction in which you are heading. Do you bring to the table what you are asking him for? Do you know what love is? Do you have a healthy measure of love? Be honest with yourself about who you are – this will give you an idea of the type of girlfriend/wife you can be.

B. **Pay attention.** His body language says it all. Don't be afraid to ask serious questions. What comes out of his mouth and what he does should always add up. Listen well enough and the truth will eventually come out. His word is *everything* and he knows it. Physical attraction isn't everything so don't pass up on guys solely based off of that. Tell him what you want – if he really likes you he will be receptive. Chivalry isn't dead although he may need your help. Maybe he didn't learn the necessary skills to properly court you but you can always teach him. Speak up for things that you don't like.

C. **It's not going to be 50/50.** You can be physically and emotionally strong, educated, and have it all together and it still wont be 50/50 – once you have accepted this, things will get easier for you. Don't be afraid to treat or pleasure him but only if you are being genuine and not because you're trying to be equal to him. When he is in tune with who he is, he will be in tune with who you are.

D. **Undo your imagination.** Don't create in your mind who you want him to be before you get to know who he really is. This can create great disappointment when the real man doesn't perform like the man you created in your mind. When you see him for who he really is then you can appreciate and enjoy his company as a person. At the same time, use your relationship as an opportunity to learn what you would like to have or not have in a partnership.

Introduction

For the majority of 2013 I tried to wrap my head around the complexities of dating. It seemed that whenever I was around my girlfriends it was only a matter of time before we would end up immersed in conversations about guys – all the things they don't do correctly, how much they don't understand us, their lack of communication, and all of the tactics that they use to try to get us into bed with them. As I started to pay more attention to conversations happening around me that other ladies were having it seemed that there was a consensus – *guys aren't shit*. But as time went on I started to analyze that notion and even tapped into my good guy friends to help me sort it out. What I realized was that they aren't actually the problem; it's us! We blame them for *everything* and rarely hold ourselves accountable when things go wrong. We are annoyed by the guy who doesn't communicate enough and also annoyed by the guy who communicates too much. We are annoyed by the guy who wants to sleep with us right away and by the guy who doesn't make a move for weeks or months. We are annoyed by the guy who doesn't open the door for us and by the guy who is extremely traditional and old fashioned in the way that he treats us. *It's time for us to cut it out!* Our confusion, sending mixed signals, and ultimately not knowing what we want has landed us a front row in the miserable dating arena.

There are plenty of good guys left; we just have to stop calling them corny, nerdy, thirsty, and boring. If we spend more time assessing where we are in life, where we want to go, what our needs are, what our pain points are, what types of people compliment our personality and what we would like to gain from an intimate relationship; our relationship success would be far greater. If we stop searching for the fantasy guy who will only exist in our heads and start giving chances to the guys who are imperfect but worth investing time in, our relationship success would be far greater. If we stop nagging and start listening, our relationship success would be far greater. If we start opening our minds before we open our legs, our relationship success would be far greater.

We have all been guilty of criticizing guys at one point or another but I hope that after you are done reading this book you will gain a different perspective on dating. While you are reading, think of me as being one of your good girlfriends who is telling you the things that you don't necessarily want to hear but need to hear. Now, since we are friends I plan on giving you nothing but the honest truth because it's only right; but I promise that my intentions are to help you. If you have any questions or wanna chat with me throughout the course of reading this book, tweet me @_missbritt2u.

I hope that you are able to laugh at yourself and relate on some level to the stories that I will share about my and my friends' experiences. My main goal is for you to challenge your views on dating and not for you to agree or disagree with me. Some chapters may apply to you while others may not, so as long as you are able to walk away with something positive and insightful after reading this I will have accomplished what I set out to. Enjoy the beginning part of the journey to opening your mind before opening your legs!

Section I:
STOP

Chapter 1

─────────

Stop Searching

It makes you look desperate! Even if you don't mind looking desperate you will never find the right one if you search for him. When you begin going places with the sole purpose of meeting a guy, you are self-sabotaging. Of course you probably aren't outwardly obvious about your intentions but it eventually overtakes your mind. It starts out innocent; you go to the movies with your girlfriends but you are secretly hoping to run into the man of your dreams while buying extra butter popcorn and a bag of Starbursts. You go out to dinner with your best friend but you are secretly hoping that the man of your dreams will walk into the restaurant, lay eyes on you and become instantly overwhelmed with lust. But then it starts to become more compulsive. You

18

go to the grocery store in your best outfit on a Saturday morning because of course; the guy you have been dreaming about will be waiting for you in aisle three! You sign up for the gym and begin scoping out the place for guys, I mean ellipticals, dressed in the best workout outfit that you could find (not to mention your hair looks great and you have no intention on sweating). You start going through your Facebook friends list to see which guys may be worth going out with. You even start to reach out to some from back in the day just to see if the flame could be relit (starts out casual but you strategically find a way to get him to take you out to dinner to "catch up"...then you pounce).

The madness has to stop! All of the time that you spend thinking of scenarios on how to meet a guy could be converted into developing a business plan, bettering your health, or getting to know who you really are. I am going to go out on a limb and say that each of us enjoys companionship and we should. Because of this I am not implying that we should sit at home and guys will start knocking on our door. We should continue socializing and hanging out with our friends with the intentions of having a great time and not meeting 'Mr. Right'. Enjoy and embrace the single life. It doesn't mean that you aren't looking for or don't want to be in a relationship, it just means that you can enjoy being by yourself without needing a guy to complete you. Besides, while you are in search mode you are more likely to force a relationship than to let it happen naturally. When relationships are forced, after the high of being in a relationship wears off, you may not be as happy as you thought you'd be.

If you enjoy searching, search to find out more about yourself – what you like, what moments make you the happiest, saddest, most inspired, etc. The more that you know about yourself the easier it will be for you to navigate through a relationship with certainty. So many of us ladies end up lost in relationships because we never even had a basic understanding of who we were. We never understood the sacrifice or compromise that it takes to remain in a healthy relationship. We never knew that we would still need our own identity no matter how wonderful the relationship may be. So please stop searching and start getting to know who you are a little better; when the time is right things will fall into place.

Chapter 2

———

Stop Assuming

You know what happens when you assume! You make an <u>ass</u> out of <u>u</u> and <u>me</u>. Assuming will only damage your relationship and your ability to ultimately communicate what is bothering you or what it is that you really want. Anyone who habitually makes assumptions will become so attached to what they have conjured up in their heads that if they were even approached with the truth they wouldn't believe it. Assumptions can stem from insecurities, lack of ability to communicate feelings, trust or control issues, or avoidance of the truth to name a few. At the same time, assuming can transform into stubbornness and bitterness if you are unwilling to listen to anyone who challenges your assumptions. You will become so attached to the story that you have created in your head that you will be blinded by what really is. We each have full control over our thoughts and should only concern ourselves with factual information.

Assuming that any guy you are dating can read your mind is silly. He does not know what you are thinking, what is bothering you, what you need him to start doing more or less of, what your needs are, or anything else that you want him to know unless you have clearly communicated it to him. Making assumptions about his behavior without knowing the truth can bring your relationship to a halt quick, fast, and in a hurry. I have yet to meet one person who enjoys being accused of doing or saying something that they did not do or say. Relying on trust and truth rather than accusations and insecurities can save you many unnecessary headaches and arguments. If you cannot bring yourself to trust the guy you are with, you are wasting his time as well as yours.

You may have never learned to confidently and articulately ask the questions necessary to receive the information that you need. Or you may be so afraid of the harsh truth that you will be confronted with after asking those questions that you simply dodge reality. Nevertheless, communication is absolutely necessary for any healthy relationship to exist. If you are unaware of how to communicate what you feel then seeking professional help may provide an immense benefit to your life. If you are purely afraid of the truth because you may end up alone and do not feel like starting the process of dating a new guy again, you are lessening what you are worth and doing yourself a disservice. Overall, assumptions can be prevented with opening clearer lines of communication, patience, and listening with the intent of understanding rather than responding.

Chapter 3

Stop Lying...To Yourself

We have all done it! And if you think you have never lied to yourself about a guy then you are lying to yourself right now. One thing that we are good at is creating layered stories with our vivid imaginations. The problem with some of the stories is that we are attempting to make an excuse or create a pass for behavior that we would not normally tolerate but have decided to for whatever reason. When we make excuses for a guy's behavior, it is because we are not willing to face the truth. We don't want to deal with the actions that would follow or conversations we will have to initiate due to his behavior. So some of us either nag or play the quiet game but we keep reassuring ourselves of the illusion that we created. Once a guy knows that he can get away with something in your presence or while being with you he will continue on per usual. And you will absolutely continue to make excuses for him until you decide to face the truth that you have been avoiding.

I met a guy recently; I'll call him Brian, who always talked about how busy and tired he was. *"Work has been so busy." "After I get out of work I am so tired and all I want to do is pass out." "My friends are inviting me to go out this weekend and I don't want to go...but I'll probably just go to show my face anyway."* The pattern I later picked up on was that what Brian was trying to do was set himself up to put in minimal effort while dating. He would continuously whine to me about his oh so busy schedule. Originally, I didn't think much of it because if I hadn't heard from him for an entire weekend I figured he was really busy. First thing Monday morning I would get a text though, *"Good Morning Beautiful. How was your weekend?"* Then I finally got it; he talked so much upfront about being busy so that I, or any one else that he was attempting to play games with, wouldn't fill in the gaps about why he was not calling or why he was giving subpar effort. We would naturally think, *"Oh he must have had a busy week at work."* Once I stopped making excuses for Brian not calling or making more of an effort I was able to see him for who he truly was. I know for a fact that, across the board, no matter how busy a person is if they really want to talk to or spend time with you they will find time and make a way with no excuses.

A friend a mine, I'll call her India, had gotten extremely accustomed to making excuses for her boyfriend Derick. Derick had, and I believe still has, major anger issues. He would constantly raise his voice at India when things weren't going his way as if she was a young child and he was her father. He was also extremely jealous and insecure and would attempt to make her feel guilty whenever she was not spending time with him; and it didn't matter if she was spending time with her family. Derick's anger and insecurity grew to a point where the rest of my friends and I refused to be around him. Anytime that any of us would talk to India about Derick and his controlling ways she would casually say, *"Guys, he's not bad all the time!"* *"Sometimes I do make him mad." "He has a right to be mad at me because you guys don't know the whole story."* It was extremely sad and frustrating to see a friend think and act as if she deserved this type of relationship. No matter how much we would tell India how pretty she was, how much she had to offer a guy, and that she deserved better the more defensive and distant she would become. After a while I realized that the distance between us was probably the best thing because I cannot make anyone see his or her truth just as someone cannot force me to see mine.

The truth is not pretty and it's not supposed to be! If we stop being so afraid of the truth and of being alone I believe that we would then stop lying to ourselves. When a guy is being honest with us, via his actions, about his situation or about the type of person he is, we need to believe him. And even aside from his behavior, women spend too much time trying to rationalize male logic instead of being accepting of their truth. Frankly, we cause a lot of our own headaches and misery in relationships. It's time to start using our imaginations to feed our creativity instead of our insecurity.

Chapter 4

━━━━━━━

Stop Settling

For anything or anyone who does not contribute to your happiness! My good friend Merieta and I were recently having a conversation about how so many of us settle in our relationships and in life in general. She kindly agreed to share some advice:

"Please stop settling and selling yourself short. It's so easy to get caught up with what we're used to but when it's not the right person for you, it only leads to heartache and wasted time. This is a road I've traveled on more than once and I finally get it! Sure, it seems like your world will crumble without him, and you may not be able to survive because he's the only one that helps you out when you need it the most. But you'll find out sooner or later that it was never a perfect

fit. Of course no one is perfect but when someone is meant for YOU they will be just right for you." – Merieta Bayati

I couldn't agree with her more. When we decide to settle, we are hindering our growth in our relationships and in life as well. We lower our standards for the sake of being with someone but how long will that relationship actually last? You will never be fulfilled because your criteria for being in a healthy relationship wasn't met. And you will probably take your frustrations out on him even though you knew before you became involved with him that he didn't have what it took to keep your interest. Don't be afraid of keeping your standards raised and of being single. Landing in a relationship because you settled can cause you to feel more alone than if you were not dating anyone. I think that most of us have a misconception of what it means and feels like to be single.

Single does not have to equate to sitting on the couch on a Friday night in sweatpants, stuffing your face with frozen pizza and Ben & Jerry's Chocolate

Fudge Brownie, listening to sulky music and looking at all of your friends and their boyfriends have fun via social media updates. All single means is that you have not found the right guy to invest time in; you do not have to become miserable and desperate because of this. I actually believe that it is wiser to remain single and actively date to get to know what you like and don't like when it comes to a relationship, as opposed to settling because you don't want to be single. Think about how you feel when one of your best friends settles for a guy – I'm sure all you can think is, *"She can do so much better; he doesn't deserve her!"* I feel the same way about you. You can do so much better so please stop settling!

Chapter 5

Stop Chasing

If he is interested he will make every effort to show you! He will call, text, or email you consistently, make it a priority to take you out and show you off, make time to get to know you – his actions will show you just how interested he is...or isn't. There is no need for you to chase him or make excuses for why he doesn't seem interested. He did not lose his cell phone the morning after you gave him your number; he just wasn't that interested. His sudden long hours at work are not the reason that he hasn't sent you a message in days; he has other priorities and getting to know you isn't one of them. He hasn't asked you out to dinner again because there may be someone else he enjoys going out to dinner with more, not because you said something crazy after two and a half glasses of vino. And all of these things are okay – everyone is not for everyone. No matter how much you like a guy who does not seem interested in you please don't get upset; there is someone out there who will make it the top of his priority list to assist you in being genuinely happy.

Chasing a guy includes, but is not limited to: a) texting him all throughout the day even though he barely responds, b) liking and commenting on 75-80% of his pictures/statuses on his social media sites, c) calling or texting him to ask why he hasn't called you, d) showing up to his job (although this may be categorized as stalking), e) "accidentally" bumping into him at his favorite restaurant (also stalking-like behavior), f) asking him where he sees things going between you two midway into the first date, g) pulling his teeth to hang out with you. Be patient, be confident, and remain poised. You are not tricking him with any of your chasing tactics – it screams, "She's crazy!" You have to remain open but mysterious – if you show him all of your cards up front what is the sense in him playing the rest of the hand? Do not take it personally if things aren't going according to how you had envisioned. It could be bad timing for him, he could be engulfed in making a career change, maybe he hasn't healed from his past relationship, perhaps he does not want to be in a committed relationship; whatever the reason, respect that he isn't interested and move on. You do not want to get in the habit of making excuses for his actions because it will spiral into much larger and complicated problems for you down the road.

No matter how much of a 'catch' you are not every guy that you meet will want to be hooked in. It is not up to you to go around promoting how great of a girlfriend or wife you will be one day; let him start the investigation process on his own. We have all been guilty of chasing at one point or another. Including me; *he was just too sexy and I couldn't help but send him that email and look through hundreds of his pictures on Instagram praying that I didn't double tap – and I didn't mean to stop by his job; TOTALLY JOKING...only about stopping by his job!* You should not let his disinterest devalue your worth or his interest validate your worth; only you hold that confirmation.

Chapter 6

Stop Being Desperate

It makes you less appealing! There is nothing attractive about being dependent on a guy, rearranging your entire life for the fear of losing him, or acting as if you need a guy to make you happy. The more desperate you are the more distracted you are by truth, happiness, and what you deserve. Once a guy realizes that you are desperate, he will either flee as fast as he can or manipulate you and play on your weaknesses. I do not believe that relationships are 50/50 all of the time because someone always puts in "more" than the other or tries a little harder to makes things work. In the end if you are truly happy and care about one another I believe that everything balances out. If you find yourself giving far more effort and energy than the guy you are with simply because you are desperate and don't want to

35

be single, you should analyze your eagerness and work on diminishing it.

There are many subtle and exaggerative signs of desperation some of which include calling, texting, and emailing entirely too much, always wanting to spend time with him, dropping your friendships, always looking for validation and fishing for compliments, constantly buying gifts for him because you think they will make him stay, acting as if you are incapable of doing something without him, agreeing with everything that he says, lowering your standards so that you won't be single, asking him to look into his crystal ball to speak to the future of your relationship before you have invested in more than one or two dates with him, constantly asking him about committing to you, making excuses for him, allowing him to get away with disrespecting you, and spending more time in relationships than being single. Just as you aren't tricking any guy with your chasing tactics, the same reins true with your desperation tactics – it screams, "She's crazy!"

Society has done a great job at pressuring us ladies to think and feel that we need to operate under the standards that 'they' have created for us; we should be married at a certain age, we should have children by a certain age, we should be seriously involved with a guy in our 20s, if we aren't seriously involved with anyone by a particular point in our lives then clearly something is wrong with us. Thus creating an illusion that subconsciously leads some to become extremely desperate to find a guy to date. If you are not seriously dating anyone by a certain time in your life where you feel like you should [and this is due to the fact that you find yourself dating the same type of guys and are getting no where], you should start dating different types of guys. If you are not seriously dating anyone by a time in your life where you feel like you should and this is due to the fact that you have been busy with your career, you should carve out time for dating. The only standards that you should follow are the ones that you have created on your own. Besides, desperately trying to find a guy will land you in a relationship where you will begin to compromise your standards. Hang in there; good guys come to those who are patient and open to receiving them.

Chapter 7

Stop Nagging

Seriously, it's annoying! Besides, nothing positive comes out of whining, I mean nagging; only a headache and most likely unresolved feelings. You see, when we nag, the focus then becomes about our nagging and not what we are nagging about. Some of you are probably laughing because you can hear yourself in your head and some of you are in denial and think that you've never been a nagger. Trust me, at some point we have all been guilty of nagging; the inner brat comes out and we want what we want when we want it. Or maybe we have been asking the same questions or mentioning the same issues over and over and feel like we haven't been heard or that we are not getting through. I know that nothing can be more frustrating than having to continually repeat ourselves but nagging is not the way to ease that frustration. We all know how to communicate and while our communication styles and our level of comfort with expressing ourselves will vary from person-to-person, we should get in the habit of using our communication skills in order to get our points across. Yes, talking, not yelling or sarcasm or huffing or puffing or the infamous silent treatment[1] but talking.

I need to point out that guys who have not yet learned how to deal with a lady who knows what she wants can misinterpret nagging. I had been casually getting to know this guy, let's call him Mason, and he would annoyingly bring up that I was nagging him. What I was actually doing was holding him to a standard that is extremely high on my list – *sticking to your word*! If you tell me that you are going to do something, do it. If you can no longer stick to your word, simply let me know. No matter how small it was, when I would call him out on not doing what he said; he would tell me that I was nagging him. This said to me that not many people had held him

---

[1] Silent Treatment (*noun*): A sometimes effective but majority of the time useless technique used by women because duh, he can obviously read our mind!

accountable for doing what he said he would do and more importantly he had not held himself accountable. Needless to say, getting to know Mason was short-lived and rightfully so. If you are communicating with tact and patience but are being told that you are nagging, more than likely there are some similarities between he and Mason; proceed with caution.

Extreme power lies in words and we should never forget that; sometimes less is more. If we can be completely honest here, we have to admit that we have a tendency of packing in lots of details, hypothetical scenarios, stories, and emotion into what was supposed to be a simple statement or question:

> *"I feel like you spend too much time at work and not enough time with me. It would be nice if you could maybe take a day off here and there so that we can spend more time together. How would you feel if I worked all the time and didn't make time for you? In order for a relationship to work two people have to be*

fully committed. If you are not willing to meet me half way then I don't even know why we are together. I do care about you and I enjoy your company but I've been thinking a lot lately and I just don't know anymore. When we first started dating it seemed like all we did was spend time together. We would go to dinner or the movies and you would do and say such cute things. You would text me "Good Morning Beautiful" and now you don't even text me good morning anymore; I'm lucky if you reply back to me during the day. I know that you are busy with work but all it takes is two seconds to reply to a text; is that too much to ask for?"

And then we wonder why he never took that day off from work – he was confused because it went from A to Z in no time! We have to be clear and concise in our communication and try to get across one point at a time. I am not in any way saying that guys need to be spoken to like they don't understand English; it's just that they are wired differently than we are (more about this later) and process information in a different way than we do so we need to be cognizant of this.

It is not too late to change your nagging ways! When you feel the irritation bubbling up inside of you, just take a deep breath before you start speaking again or even walk away if you have to (later on, you both will be happy that you did). Continuous nagging will only push your guy away and as I said earlier, will leave you with nothing but a headache and unresolved feelings.

Chapter 8

Stop The Cycle

Don't let it go on any longer! Our attitudes, fears, and behaviors when it comes to being in relationships almost always link back to our childhoods. We gauged our sense of "normalcy" by what we saw and the environment(s) in which we spent most of our time. As we became more observant of our surroundings and developed our own ideals about the world of relationships, we either wanted to mirror what we saw or change it...and fast. The unfortunate reality for many of us is that once we decided that we wanted to create a more suitable set of criteria than what we were exposed to early on, our subconscious mind had already stored the attitudes, fears, and behaviors that we so desperately wanted to change. This is not to say that the majority of us grew up in unruly or dysfunctional households but perhaps we saw the disruption or anger caused by financial burdens, a lack of communication, support, respect, affection, romance, responsibility, passion, togetherness, smiling, or a combination thereof.

Stopping the cycle can be a painful process due to the memories that our pasts may force us to relive but it is so necessary that we heal and create a more soothing way forward. We absolutely need to assess our relationships with our fathers, our parents' relationships with each other, our parents' relationships with their parents, our family dynamic, and our past relationships with guys. We should look for any parallels or patterns that negatively impact our ability to sustain happy and healthy relationships. We will then need to remain aware of these parallels and patterns and how they impact our thought processes, interactions, standards, beliefs and attitudes.

One of the many cycles that I have decided to stop is the 'dominate woman in relationships' syndrome (yes, I made that up). I come from a family of very strong-willed women, which is both inspiring and disconcerting. Seeing the women in my family exude confidence, handle the toughest situations with poise then balance family, work, and play while making it look effortless; all the while still being able to remain honest, altruistic, and morally conscious is truly, truly inspiring. Because of these women I have developed an 'I can be anything, I can do anything, I can get through anything' attitude which I am extremely grateful for. In the same token, I saw these same women completely dominate relationships – wearing the pants so to speak. The guys were needy, didn't take initiative, were looking for another mom to take care of them, weren't communicative, could never get a word out in a disagreement, and hadn't quite graduated into Manhood despite their age. I thought that was normal! Besides, nurturing and taking initiative come natural to me. After encountering several of these guys while dating I realized that something didn't feel right. I would ask my girlfriends, "Why am I *always* taking the initiative? Why doesn't he have any drive or ambition? Doesn't he want more out of life? Aren't guys supposed to be hunters and go after what they want?"

The answer to the last is yes, guys do go after what they want whether it be finding someone to take care of them or finding someone who they can build a future with. I realized that instead of asking my friends those questions about guys I needed to be asking myself a few questions instead; *"Why are you settling for a guy that doesn't take initiative? Why are you investing time in a guy that doesn't have any drive or ambition? Don't you want more out of relationships? If guys go after what they want don't you feel like you can just have fun with dating and let a guy show you what he's about?"* I decided that I did not want to be dominating in my intimate relationships but rather I wanted a guy to take control. At least one of you is thinking, "So she wants to be submissive? Won't be me!" No, I'm not saying that I want to submit myself to a guy; I do find comfort and reassurance in masculine energy though and when he is not afraid to take control of a situation. I have also come to understand the negative effects of a guy feeling as though he is not needed, that he cannot provide, and when his ego is not being caressed. Of course I will never suppress my voice – I will speak up for myself, never tolerate disrespect, and put my foot down when I feel the need to but I will not embrace the 'dominate woman in relationships' syndrome.

The cycles that each of us will want to stop, or have worked to stop already, will vary in complexity, pain, and the time it takes to reverse them but please do not be discouraged. We owe it to ourselves to learn from our past oversights and those of our parents, grandparents, and family. Stopping the cycle is about us all becoming aware of the behaviors and attitudes that have already or have the potential to plague our relationship success and working to change them for the better.

Chapter 9

Stop Blaming Him For Your Emotional Voids

It is not your fault that your dad wasn't there! And it is not any other guy's fault either. After reading the previous chapter I know that everyone will start or continue to work on stopping the cycle, right? But in the meantime please do not blame any guy that you are dating for your emotional voids, or what is better known as "daddy issues". Before I go on I should point out that not each of us has daddy issues. Some of your dads have been a continuous provider, emotional support system, and a backbone for you; so while the majority of this chapter may not apply to you, I know that there are so many ladies who need to hear this message.

Fatherless parenting can be broken down into three categories: a child who never knew or met their father, a child whose father was in and out of their life (financially, emotionally, physically), or a child who lived with their father but he did not provide any nurturing or emotional support. No matter what category you fall into, the emotional void can cut just as deep. Reflecting on how the wounds of being a fatherless child have impacted you will most certainly be a painful and emotional process, trust me, I've gone through the process myself and am continuing to stay attentive to my pain points. I fall into the second category of fatherless parenting; I have some really great memories of spending time with my dad and have learned several invaluable lessons from him and I have some really unpleasant memories as well. I will not use this or any other platform to bash or "expose" him, however, I hope that I can use what I have learned to help at least one of you reading this. I have learned that:

- Parenting is the most difficult job ever known to man

- Its difficulty does not give any parent a pass to

not take care of or to be in and out of the lives of their children

- Holding onto anger and pain will cause YOU the most detriment
- There is no excuse big enough that could warrant a father not being there for his daughter (or son)
- It is not your fault
- You deserve to be loved and to love yourself
- Your father is your first male role model
- If you use sex as a remedy to your daddy issues you will have far more issues than you initially started out with
- How your father treated your mom and how he treated you subconsciously formed your initial beliefs of what love looked like
- Regardless of which category of fatherless parenting that you fall into, and no matter how old you get, you will always (and sometimes secretly and deep down) crave a healthy and loving relationship with your father

- You have the power within you to overcome any painful situation that you have gone through
- Parents who are not actively and emotionally involved in their children's lives are missing out...big time
- Forgiveness should be atop of your life's priority list
- Forgive your father – if he knew better, he'd do better (if you think he knows better forgive him anyway). Forgiveness is for you, not him
- There is always room for repair (whether the repair is by yourself or with your father)

I can imagine that the vast majority of us never stopped dating due to not receiving the type of love that we so desperately needed from our fathers. With this, we have all blamed another guy at one point or another for what our fathers said or didn't say, or what he did or didn't do – please stop! We need to first be honest with ourselves about our voids and be sure that we are not displacing our frustrations or hurt onto someone else.

If your father always told you that he would pick you up and take you to get ice cream but would never show up, please do not chew the head off of the guy who cancelled a date (if he continuously cancels that is a completely different story). If your father was never there, please do not push away the guy who is genuinely trying to get to know you. If your father was never there, please do not get mad at your boyfriend because he is not showing you attention 24/7; you do not have to be attached at the hip – learn to give yourself attention. If your father always forgot your birthday, please do not give the silent treatment to your boyfriend because he bought you flowers and your favorite candy but didn't take you out to the restaurant that you had been hinting at, for two weeks prior, that you wanted him to take you to. Be responsible and take accountability for your voids – it is not anyone else's responsibility except yours to nurture that hurt little girl that lives inside of you. And if your father was there for you and created a close to perfect example of what type of guy you should be dating, please do not make any guy feel as if he will never be able to satisfy 'daddy's little princess' if he is genuine, loves and respects you, makes you laugh, and you enjoy being in his company. More than likely your dad was raised in a different generation than the guys you would be dating and the times have clearly changed.

Aside from having daddy issues everyone in the world battles insecurities. Please do not put your insecurities off on anyone, especially on anyone you are dating because it will always be a lose-lose situation for you both. If you think you have gained weight do not put him in an awkward situation and ask him if he thinks your jeans still fit – watch what you eat or begin a workout regime. If you do not feel pretty on a particular day do not ask him if he thinks you are attractive – of course he does or he wouldn't be spending time with you. If you have been cheated on before do not go through his phone, stalk all of his social media sites looking for pictures that he's commented on, and read his email trying to find information; instead, ask questions and use your intuition. If you are feeling lonely that's okay – spending time by yourself is healthy and certainly necessary; he doesn't need to rescue you every time you feel bored or alone. We should all communicate what we need, ask for what we want, have patience, and respect the guy who tries.

Lastly, parallel to daddy issues are mommy issues. I find that people don't talk about them a lot – maybe it's the discomfort of acknowledging or presenting a truth about the woman who carried us for nine months that keeps the topic hushed. But many women have mommy issues as well. Never receiving love, nurture, or emotional support from the one woman who is always supposed to have your back and know you the best can hurt pretty badly. Maybe your mom abandoned you (physically, emotionally or spiritually). Maybe your mom always placed importance on men and not her children. Maybe she was abusive, or dismissive, or angry, or unsure of the direction her life was supposed to go in and so her life was always in disarray. *Forgive her!* As women, our dads show us how we should be treated while our moms show us how to treat ourselves. If we disagree with the examples they've set we have some reestablishing to do.

Section II:
R-E-S-P-E-C-T

Chapter 10

Have It, Show It, Give it, Get It

THIS IS SO IMPORTANT IT DESERVES CAPITAL LETTERS and a section all by itself! Respecting yourself and your body is so very important. The level of respect that you have for yourself indicates to *anyone* that you come in contact with how to treat, speak to and approach you. There will certainly be people who cross you the wrong way but remember you have control over what you will and will not tolerate. You've probably heard this before but a guy will only do what you allow him to do. You have to teach a guy how to respect you: the appropriate way to communicate with you, how to never cross your established boundaries, how to earn and then not break your trust, how to honor your independence, how to crave, appreciate, and satisfy but never disrespect your body, how to never belittle you, how to not ignore your point(s) of view or beliefs, etc.

When we first meet a guy his perspective on how to approach and thereafter treat us is based off of what he saw growing up, his relationship with his mom and dad (his parents' relationship), society, and what his previous girlfriends have allowed. Regardless of what he has been previously exposed or used to we will always have to teach him how to treat us. And as a side note, respect is definitely mutual! If this sounds like a lot, it's because we complicate things when it comes to the opposite sex. Think back to when you initially met some of your best friends. Ahh the memories! You were inseparable and all you could think about was having fun and spending more time together. You can be the same way with the guys you are dating (you can decide on the levels of inseparability). You didn't probe your best friends with hundreds of questions about their pasts the first time you hung out. You didn't come to dinner with a list of dos and don'ts; you just enjoyed their company. I clearly understand the differences between the two types of relationships but we tend to think that we have more to lose when it comes to intimate relationships than we do with our closest friendships but I'd like to challenge that – friendships can be even more intimate based on our extreme vulnerability. We share...sometimes even overshare the most intricate details of our lives with our friends. If they were to betray us, we would be ultimately hurt. We have arguments, forgive one another and go back to being best of friends. While what we require from our best friends tends to be understood but unspoken there are a plethora of similarities in what we require from the guys we date.

This may sound cliché and cheesy at best but your body is truly a temple. You are **not** a sex object, **not** a toy, **not** someone who should be used and put back onto the shelf, **not** a physical (or verbal) punching bag. Your beauty is **not** determined by the size of your boobs. Your worth is **not** measured by your physical attraction. Your body is **not** your best asset. You are worth more than after hour calls for sex. How you dress tells guys which category to put you in. When I say how you dress I mean how much skin you're showing. Regardless of if a guy is looking for a serious relationship, when he first meets you he will decide at first glance whether you are the type that he can introduce to his mother or if you are the type he will only text at 3:15am for a quickie. When you are showing a lot of skin I am not saying that you deserve to be disrespected or treated like a doormat; it's just that how you carry yourself and how you are dressed will determine how guys will approach and speak to you. The respect that you have for yourself should be reflected in the type of clothes that you wear. If you do not want purely sexual attention from guys please dress accordingly. Now don't go and replace your wardrobe with turtlenecks and sweatpants; you can show skin and still look classy. Respect yourself or no guy ever will.

Section III:
Ask Yourself These Questions

Chapter 11

A Dollar For A Dollar?

Check your wallet! Many times we have our standards laid out on the table accompanied by napkins, cutlery, champagne flutes, wine glasses, water cups, an array of appetizers, and an elegant centerpiece. So picturesque! But can you mirror what you have laid out? For example, is one of your standards that a guy has to be healthy, have a six-pack and work out every week but your running sneakers have been collecting dust in the trunk of your car right next to that crumbled up McDonald's bag? Or that he has to make over six figures but your salary doesn't come close to that? Or that he needs to be respectful but you don't even respect yourself? Or that he needs to have a five-year plan and you have yet to set your goals for this year? Or that he needs to be supportive but you are not the type to encourage or lift someone up when they need it the most? Or that he has to give you back-to-back orgasms but you have a long list of "Ew, sorry but I don't do that!" Or that he needs to be a positive person but negative energy seems to follow you around wherever you go? Or that he must be an honest person but you are never honest and upfront about how you feel or what you want? There is nothing wrong with wanting an upgrade; just make sure you upgrade yourself too.

There's a woman I went to high school with who expects a guy to court her if they are dating. She wasn't very specific but I will assume that she meant things like opening doors, paying for dinner, and pulling out her chair. Just making sure that you are all still paying attention – no assuming, remember? Regardless of her definition of courtship, I realized that whenever she went out to bars or clubs her boobs were always showing and her dresses were very, *very*, short. In addition, if I had to caption the majority of the pictures that she would post on Facebook and Instagram it would read, "Please like my picture, I am in desperate need of attention #desperate #attention #likethis". She would also post tons of sexual innuendos that hinted at what she enjoyed most about her sexual encounters (how rough she liked it and how wet she can get). In between posting pictures about sex and of going out in her club attire she would post her frustrations that "there are no good men left". Although there isn't anything wrong with liking and enjoying attention, desperately searching for it will end in an emotional disaster. I mentioned to her that if I were a guy looking at the pictures that she posted on social media, courtship would not be the first idea that would come to mind. Her standard of wanting a guy to respect her conflicted with the fact that she didn't have enough respect for herself. Her standard of wanting a guy to court her conflicted with the fact that she constantly exuded sex both in public and online, which leaves nothing to a guy's imagination. I was just trying to look out for her but she didn't enjoy hearing my opinion – oops!

Whatever your standards are they should be comparable to what you bring to the table. I believe that we each should have high (but realistic) standards with the ability to match everything that we anticipate receiving. The whole point of setting standards is so that we can easily identify those who possess the qualities that mean the most to us and are high on our lists, and avoid those who have a drastically different set of standards and beliefs.

Chapter 12

Is It Time To Call A Locksmith?

Do you know when the locks need to be changed? Do you know when it's time to shut the door and move on? Most of us are so caught up in our standards that we forget to factor in what is non-negotiable; what are we not willing to compromise on? Depending on what we are looking for at a particular time we may incorporate wiggle room into our standards but our non-negotiable list should never waver. One of my preferences, for example, is to date a guy who has no children. I *love* children but I understand and respect that having a child is a major responsibility. Because I have no children of my own (and I plan to keep it this way for a bit longer), I know that if I were to seriously date a guy who has a child we would have conflicting priorities. And might I add the occasional unresolved issues with the child's mother – very sticky! There is wiggle room, however. I would never dismiss a guy I enjoyed being around solely because he had a child, especially if he was a responsible and active parent. I would also go out on a date with a guy if he told me upfront that he had a child – I would see what he was about and if he and I had similar standards/beliefs. I also understand that as I get older the percentage of guys that have children will increase and consequently I will have to become more flexible. On the other hand, there are other areas in which I have no wiggle room. One non-negotiable of mine is inconsistency – it drives me nuts hence the reason it is a non-negotiable. By inconsistency I mean doing one thing and saying another, not following through, and not being true to who [they] are regardless of the circumstance or who is around. Another non-negotiable of mine is continual dishonesty. When someone is comfortable lying to themselves they will be that much more comfortable lying to everyone else. I consider myself to be an upright person and I love the truth even if it's messy and won't feel too good initially; I cannot associate with anyone who does not share the same sentiments.

While we will each have dissimilar non-negotiable lists the point is that we have a list. Never lose sight of the instances or behaviors that you consider to be not acceptable. The moment that you begin to rearrange your non-negotiable list you are simultaneously sacrificing your happiness and sanity. When you are in love or have invested quite a bit of time into the guy you are seeing it may be more difficult for you to walk away; just know that while it may be difficult, you are disrespecting yourself by accepting behaviors that you think are intolerable. So don't be afraid to call the locksmith, there may be a much more sturdy and reliable lock waiting to replace the old one.

Chapter 13

Will I Be Aroused If My Cognition Is Stroked?

Will you scream? Will you moan? Will your legs start to shake? Your mind should be caressed before you give up the cookies. If he can't seem to find your spot via intellectual and stimulating conversation, he does not deserve the opportunity to pleasure your other spot. I've heard that the way to a man's heart is through his stomach – I think the way to a lady's cookie is through her mind. But if he is eager to feed your mind please make sure you have an appetite. A guy should be able to stimulate you emotionally and intellectually before sexually, and you should require that of him. And if he can't then he does not deserve to dip your warm cookie in his milk. I think that sex has lost its importance in our society due to the fact that 'sex sells' and we have become oversold on sex via movies, TV, music, magazines, advertising/marketing, and the internet. It is up to each of us though to individually place the value back into sex. I'm not saying to take the cookies off the shelf completely because realistically you'd be punishing yourself too. All I'm saying is to put the cookies on a higher shelf so they aren't as easy to grab – allow him to get a ladder. If he is too lazy to get a ladder he is not the right guy for you. If he gets the ladder but isn't genuine about climbing (you know, he's climbing just so that he can get some cookies then he's off to the next cookie jar) then he is not the guy for you.

This is not just about sex though, we have to do a better job at being vulnerable with our clothes on – pillow talking without the pillows – allowing ourselves to be naked before we undress – requiring that our mind be given the first orgasm. Sex is not just a physical act; it encompasses emotional connection, trust, vulnerability, and openness (no pun). The problem lies not just in the fact that sex has lost its importance but that sex has become so casual a.k.a. the notorious "friends with benefits". My mind can't [intentionally] seem to recollect if I've ever been in a friend with benefits situation but I do know (from my friends of course) that while you *think* you are 'benefitting' you are only hurting yourself in the end. If you continuously have casual sex with minimal standards what will happen when you decide that you want more? He most certainty won't like the switch up. How will you put the cookies on a higher shelf after having them at eye-level for so long? Will you feel comfortable when a guy reaches for a ladder? Will you feel comfortable with the vulnerability and emotions that come with being naked with your clothes on? The longer that you engage in casual sex the longer you will not benefit – don't be fooled. The energy we put out comes back.

I met a guy, who I'll call Arthur, while I was out to lunch one day. He started making small talk and asked me if I would go out for drinks with him. Arthur seemed nice so we exchanged numbers and soon after he invited me out to dinner. I wouldn't say that dinner was a complete disaster but I was a little turned off by a few of his comments. The next evening he texted me and asked if I wanted to come over his house and "hang out" – I couldn't believe that he somehow thought that cookies were on the table. Even more so, I couldn't believe that his 'come hang out' line had worked previously (if it hadn't he would have never felt comfortable enough to use it with me). Needless to say my cookies were out of his reach. Not necessarily because we only went out one time, more because he had no real intention of getting to know me let alone trying to stimulate me intellectually.

"A mind is a terrible thing to waste" so please do not waste it. Allow a guy to challenge your thoughts and engage your psyche in thought-provoking conversations. Once he has done so he will have a higher level of appreciation and understanding of who you are – and you will have a higher level of appreciation and understanding of whom you are giving yourself to. Having your mind stroked can be even more intimate than the act of sex and trust me it can get hot and heavy. Your cookies belong on a higher shelf until someone is willing to reach for them but not just because he is hungry and likes eating cookies; but because he knows you are worth reaching for. I know a 'girl's got needs too' but open your mind before you open your legs!

And since we're talking about cookies, it is important that you know the difference between what we are thinking when we give up the cookies for the first time and what he is thinking after he licks the first crumbs off his fingers. I truly believe that our mind should be given the first orgasm thus our emotional attachment to him begins before we open our legs. Just know that the relationship begins for him after he's tasted that snickerdoodle for the first time! Sure, you may be in a committed relationship before you decide to give it up but his emotional attachment begins after you've connected sexually. You may emotionally arouse him before becoming physically intimate, however, his deeper attachment comes thereafter. Just something for you to think about – I don't make the rules!

Chapter 14

Why Do Airlines Charge $75 If My Bag Is Overweight?

Because you are carrying too much 'stuff'! There is nothing amusing about bringing loads of baggage into a new relationship. There is also nothing wrong with taking time to heal and better yourself before jumping into a new relationship. He does not want to constantly hear about what your ex-boyfriend did or didn't do; I promise! Each of us should weigh our baggage before attempting to deal with someone new. Do you have severe insecurities that you need to work on? Do you have unresolved and unattended daddy issues (see chapter 9)? Are you afraid of or not ready for commitment? Are you overwhelmed with your priorities? Are you paranoid that every guy you date will cheat on you? Are you obsessed with the sound of your ticking biological clock? Did something tragic and/or unexpected happen in your family and you need time to make sense of it all?

You are not fooling anyone because your suitcase is cute and fashionable, whatever is inside still needs to be examined...and weighed. The reality is that we all come into relationships with some baggage; the key is to be responsible and make sure that we are emotionally stable enough to intimately welcome someone new into our lives. It is irresponsible and selfish to know that we should take time out for ourselves but instead we ignore it because a) we are lonely, b) he is just too good-looking to pass up, c) self-reflection is not the easiest thing in the world, d) again, we are lonely, or e) none of the above but time heals everything, right?

My grandmother would always tell me to pack extra clothes for vacation because I never knew what would come up or what adventures I'd go on; she'd say it's better to overpack and have more clothes than to have to go shopping while on vacation. And let's be honest – a bag full of cute outfits and pairs of shoes never hurt anyone! I don't want to make a generalization but many of us tend to overpack (our trip is for three days and we have one main bag with clothes, a separate bag for toiletries, a purse, and a medium bag with that extra pair of shoes that didn't fit in our main bag plus a small bag for our hair supplies and jewelry). Then on the last day of the trip we *finally* recognize that we packed too much 'stuff'. Overpacking may be a natural or learned routine for many of us but we all need to remain aware of what we have packed before heading into a new relationship. We all need to think about the bags that we are holding onto and get rid of the extra baggage (no, we should not put all of our smaller bags into the bigger bag).

Chapter 15

Are Red Capes For Bulls Only?

Should they be the only ones who react when they see a red flag? Red flags are essentially the behaviors or conversations that raise caution inside of us – they say, "something just doesn't feel right!" It's when our intuition is alerting us that we need to either reassess our current situation or that we need to avoid creating a risky situation. We have all been guilty of ignoring or not recognizing red flags at one time or another but we have to do a better job at remaining mindful. Think of a red flag as a free hint – a clue – a sign that we need to go back and review our standards. In the event that we ignore one red flag, we will be presented with another red flag, then another red flag, then another red flag and eventually we will have a red cape covered with red tape. When the bull finally comes charging at us we become overwhelmed, angry, and sometimes even spiteful. But how can we be mad at the bull if we have all of the red flags in our hand? The bull that comes charging at us is all of the instances that we ignored blowing up in our face. We are responsible for staying alert and listening to our intuition so that we can protect ourselves from the bull.

If any of you are like me you can commiserate with me regarding my anal-retentive nature of needing to know everything and how it fits in with the direction I'm headed in. I have been working on it (I swear) although I have to admit that in the past it was difficult for me to embrace a red flag. I would recognize it then because I didn't know how the red flag would translate or what it actually meant I would keep on as if I never saw it. In those times I was hindering myself because I was essentially ignoring behavior(s) that didn't feel right solely because I didn't know what it would mean down the road. Believing that everyone deserves a second chance would also hinder my ability to react to a red flag. For example, Brian (whom I mentioned earlier in Chapter 3) showed plenty of red flags and insecurities when I first met him but because I didn't know what it would mean later on I didn't address them right away. He would always talk about his ex-girlfriends (red flag); and how so many ladies wanted him therefore he never had to work hard at the dating scene (red flag); and how he believed that he brought so much to the table *solely* because he was good looking, had a job, a car, and his own place (insecurity); and how he wasn't used to someone like me...you know, having standards and all (red cape).

It wouldn't be right if I didn't address how much we like to give the benefit of the doubt in part because we believe so strongly that we can fix guys. *We have to stop!* Guys are not projects for us to "fix". They are human, just like us; they have feelings, just like us; they want to be happy in a relationship; just like us. Giving the benefit of the doubt is only detrimental when we are 1) doing so because we have a plan on how we will create the 'perfect' man out of him, 2) ignoring red flags and giving too much 'benefit' and being left with too much 'doubt', and 3) sticking around and being overly nurturing in hopes that he will one day change. Red flags exist for a reason – for us to make a mental note and to protect ourselves from misery down the road. Even if you cannot make sense of a red flag when it occurs if something feels off then it probably is. Learning to use our rational minds rather than our emotions to make decisions will also help us with being able to identify and react to red flags. Listen to yourself and don't be afraid to walk away.

Chapter 16

Am I Looking For Ken?

Human or plastic? Let's be real Ken is hot – perfect hair, perfect abs, perfect eyes, perfect lips, perfect with his clothes on...and off (you undressed your dolls too!). But how much fun would it be to date Ken? Quite frankly he'd be boring. If he were perfect then there would be no room for growth and nothing to look forward to. But so many of us are looking for Ken – the fantasy of having the perfect guy, the perfect relationship, the white picket fence and four-car garage. I hate to be the bearer of bad news but Ken does not exist in real life. The ideal guy that we have created in our mind does not exist in real life. The guy who has chocolate waiting on a platter for us during that time of the month does not exist in real life. The guy who never disappoints us does not exist in real life. The guy who can mysteriously read our mind does not exist in real life. The guy who has no insecurities does not exist in real life. The guy who won't at least subliminally hint at fellatio during that time of the month does not exist in real life. The guy who would rather go shopping with us instead of watching football on Sunday, playing golf, and/or hanging out in his man cave with his friends does not exist in real life. But the guy who is imperfect, makes mistakes but has pure intentions, is worth fighting for, and puts substantial effort into making us happy does exist in real life.

When we become obsessed with Ken in our minds we are absolutely dismissing guys right in front of us who have potential. We look at the guy who is a gentleman and tell him that he is too nice. We look at the guy who is expressive and tell him that he's not tough enough. We look at the guy who opens doors and tell him he's corny. We look at the guy who constantly communicates and enjoys hanging out with us and call him "thirsty". We look at the guy who has strong faith and we want him to loosen up. And when I hear my guy friends say that some ladies are impossible to please, I have to agree. We can become so overly critical and obsessive that we will never be happy. If you find yourself constantly rejecting guys because "he isn't good enough" you should either stop interacting with the same type of guys or realize that you are the problem. There are plenty of great guys out there but if you are only looking for Ken, and Ken only, you are blinding yourself to reality. Broaden your dating horizons – start dating guys who you normally wouldn't be interested in. What's the worst that could happen? No matter if you go out on one date or five you will not only learn something about him but about yourself as well. Leave Ken for Barbie!

Section IV:

Just So You Know

Chapter 17

Crack Open Your Head And Take A Look

Your mind is so sexy! Much, much sexier than your body! Physical appearance may be the first thing that catches the eye but intellectual conversation is such a turn on. Your looks can only hold a guy's attention but for so long – your mind on the other hand can hold his attention for far longer (conversation, your thought process, how you analyze information, your advice/suggestions). I see so many ladies in the gym, going on diets, and trying to find the quickest way to lose weight all to enhance their physical appearance. I have even had some friends who are my age hint at their interest in minor Botox. I wonder how many of those ladies are just as interested in reading a book, learning more about life or themselves, or exploring the world to experience different cultures. While I do think that our physical health and appearance is important, our mental health should not be disregarded – our mind needs exercise, stimulation, and rejuvenation as well. Looks are not everything – I repeat, *looks are not everything*! Guys who are looking for substance will need more than a pretty face to look at everyday. Don't be afraid of showcasing your intellect.

I once had a guy tell me on a date, "You are so smart it's almost intimidating" – I couldn't believe it! Intimidating? *Why?* He didn't feel secure enough within himself to explore his intellectual desires; which led to his inability to accept and embrace my need for feeding my brain. Because of this, he felt as if he could not hold a stimulating conversation with me. Still, I didn't let his comment deter me from being myself. I would never presumptuously hold a conversation; however, there is an instinctive need within me to engage in thought provoking and stimulating conversation and I will never ignore that need.

A few ways that I enjoy exercising my mind is by having conversation, solving Sudoku puzzles, playing Connect Four (yes, there is strategy involved), setting goals, listening to music and simultaneously reading the lyrics, experiencing something for the first time, reading, writing (clearly), and by driving so that I can organize my thoughts. Your list may completely differ from mine but please do not downplay or overlook the importance of keeping your mind sexy. There is no piece of clothing or jewelry you can buy that can give you more confidence than your thoughts can. *Let your appearance compliment your mind not vice versa.* There is much more to you than what everyone sees on the surface, let all of you shine through!

Chapter 18

━━━━━━━━━

Clocks Were Invented For A Reason

So that we could keep track of our most valuable asset! Time is something that we can never get back. Once the moment is done, it's done. Once the day is over, it's over. With this, think back to how much time that you have spent in relationships ignoring red flags, lowering your standards, trying to create Ken, nagging, and lying to yourself? I tend to think that there is no such thing as "wasted time" because every situation, interaction, and conversation that we have is a learning experience; we should still remain conscious of who we are investing time in though. This is not to say that within a relationship there won't be ups and downs. In any healthy relationship there will be plenty of both although there is a difference between investing time in a guy who shows you respect and appreciation than in a guy who does not.

Your time is so precious please guard it and be careful about who you are compromising it for. Those who do not appreciate your time don't deserve you – your energy, your company, your conversation, your attention, and definitely not your cookie. Allocating your time can be problematic if you think too much about it though. That may sound like a contradiction. How can I suggest for you to be careful about whom you are investing time in and in the same breath suggest that you shouldn't think too much about investing your time? Knowing that my time is a valuable asset, I would sometimes rule out guys very quickly based off of something they said or did because I was so afraid of wasting my time; even though I had/have standards and could spot a red flag based off of them. Those instances became problematic for me because I was spending so much *time* thinking about whether I was wasting my *time* that I wasn't allowing situations to play out organically – I wasn't living in the 'now'. I will caution you about becoming too infatuated with your time all the while still respecting it.

With any investment comes risk – sometimes our investments are spot on and at times they may be off course. But if there is no risk there can be no reward. We should also remain aware of what we are looking for and align our investments accordingly. For instance, if I am in need of urgent cash I may day-trade in the stock market to see if I can make money. If I will be in need of cash a year or two from now I may invest in longer-term stocks so that I can make money over time. Investing time is no different. If I am looking for a serious relationship I need to invest time in guys who are also looking for a serious relationship. If I am only looking to sporadically date for a while just to have fun and learn more about what I like and dislike about relationships, I need to invest time in guys who are looking for the same. This is not to say that feelings and desires won't change but initially aligning our investments will save us many troubles.

Chapter 19

====

All Guys Are Not

— — — — —

Fill in the blank with whatever you think all guys are. This is the topic that inspired me to write this book. I often hear so many ladies sitting around talking about "guys aren't this", "guys aren't that", "all guys are dogs", "all guys cheat", "all guys want is sex", "all guys are dumb", "all guys aren't shit" – I used to be one of those ladies too. What I have learned is that all guys are not what we have experienced in the past, good or bad. The reason that you still think that 'all guys are...' is because you keep dealing with the same type of guys. If I can be bluntly honest, now that I am enlightened it is extremely irritating to hear the complaining, whining, negativity and bitterness about what all guys are – I can only imagine what I sounded like. It's time to stop generalizing guys! It's also time to stop dealing with guys who are dogs, who cheat, who only want sex, who are "dumb", and who aren't shit. I will point out that what I mean by all guys not being dogs is that not every guy will dog you out. I do believe though that there is a dog that lives within every male. Each of those dogs is not aggressive by any means; it's not possible (not every dog has the same intimidation factor as say a Pit Bull or a Rottweiler). They all bark though and they still have teeth – never deny them of that.

Making negative generalizations about guys will surely interrupt your ability to meet a good one. In the event that a good guy approaches you, you will be so attached to your "all guys are..." belief that you would not be able to recognize what great qualities he has to offer. Categorizing all guys with a negative connotation will make you appear bitter. There is nothing wrong with coming to the realization that you have dated guys who have played games, played you, and have brainwashed you to believe they were someone that they weren't. If we could all be truthful – we have each been in a situation where our emotions have been toyed with and taken for granted. The key is to become more aware of who we are sharing vulnerable moments with and not to write off all guys completely.

It is easy to become bogged down with negative thoughts about dating but we are in control of our thoughts and what we allow ourselves to believe. The types of guys that you have seen family members and friends with can also impact your negative views/generalizations but it is not too late to change your perspective. I promise you that there are plenty of good guys left. Even if you haven't seen any in a long while keep the faith and maintain a positive attitude about your romantic life. Life becomes extremely enjoyable once we are open and decide to change our attitudes and perspectives. All guys are not ---!

Chapter 20

Orgasms ≠ Problem Solver

Sex is only a problem if you think it's the answer. While orgasms are great for relieving stress, bonding with a significant other, and even helping us remain healthy (according to some medical research) they do not solve problems. Sex won't make him stay. Good sex won't make him stay. Mind-blowing sex will probably get you a call back but if he is not ready to commit, sex will not solve that problem. If he hasn't been paying you much attention lately, sex will not keep his attention on you for the long-term. If he has been avoiding having that conversation you really want to have sex won't make him feel like talking. If he has been cheating and told you that it was because you haven't been "giving him any" then sex won't make him stop cheating. Sex is not supposed to be a problem solver so please do not get emotional when it does not solve your problems.

My good friend Curt and I were debating about whether sex actually solves problems and although we initially disagreed, after thinking more about it he had a change of heart. "I agree that all sex does is postpone and sidetrack what the underlying problem, issue or topic is for the moment. It's more of a deterrent in some cases. It's also an outlet for stress, emotions and tension. On top of that, it can be a way to connect with someone or satisfy your personal needs. It can also boost you up in a bad time but actually it only sidetracks your mind from the bad to the "good feeling" of it...shortly after you're back to where you were before you engaged in sex." Don't let that good feeling distract you from reality. Life will throw many situations at you where you'll experience good, bad, and ambiguous feelings and as you have noticed – none of these feelings last. The climatic feeling that we [hopefully] experience during sex is also one of those feelings that do not last.

You can spend your life chasing that feeling as if it was a drug or false therapeutic security blanket *or* you can learn to solve problems without the use of escaping mechanisms. Misusing sex is no different than using drugs and alcohol to escape everyday realities. Once that good feeling fades and reality resurfaces, more drugs are taken in order to numb; tolerance increases therefore more and more drugs are taken in order to keep the avoidance at an all time high (no pun). Enjoy sex for what it is, not for what it can help you sidestep.

Chapter 21

Single Relationships Are A Blast

Have you learned how to be in one? If not you are doing yourself a huge disservice. Being in a relationship with yourself is the second most important connection in your life, the first being your faith in a higher power. If you have not learned to be happy while you are single there is no way that you will ever be happy in a relationship with anyone else. Learning to love yourself is the best love you will ever feel[2]. I have friends who jump from relationship to relationship to relationship because they don't enjoy 'the single life'. Their inability to enjoy being single

---

[2] Shameless but totally relatable plug; don't forget to pick up my first book *Loving Inward, Living Outward, Looking Forward* if you haven't already.

causes them to fall in and out of love very quickly and to never fully grasp who they are, what they like, or what they truly want.

Sadly there is stigma attached to being single – "if she hasn't found someone yet it's because she's probably crazy", "she must be single because nobody wants her", "that's why she's lonely, with her single ass"; all of which I consider nonsense. You don't have to be single and alone. I know people who have been single for years but have more 'date nights' than their friends who are in relationships. Being in a relationship does not imply that you are happy or fulfilled by default. I also know people who have felt more alone in relationships than they ever did while being single. Think of being single as a time of restoration, finding out more about yourself, and enjoying the ability to act selfishly.

One thing I have learned about happiness is that it's an inside-out process. If we have not learned to be our own friend, to love ourselves, to have fun by ourselves, or to laugh at ourselves we will fail miserably at finding a great friend, reject anyone who claims to love us, deny anyone of showing us a fun time, and become angry when we are being laughed at. Happiness starts with you and being able to find happiness in a relationship also starts with you. He is not responsible for your happiness; you are! If he makes a genuine contribution, he is a keeper. Embrace the single life no matter how badly you want to be in a relationship. If you reject being single no matter how many Mr. Right's you meet you will never be open to receive what he has to offer you. Get it out of your head that being single equates to something being wrong with you – there is nothing wrong with you...unless there is actually something wrong with you! All joking aside, don't allow anyone to convince you that your being single is mirrored by your worth. Keep your standards raised, find internal happiness and just live!

Chapter 22

You Can Open The Door

It won't kill chivalry I promise. Feeling comfortable and confident enough to take initiative in a relationship is an instrumental component of how successful the relationship will or will not be. According to my good friend Nick, "A lady that takes initiative in a relationship or the beginning stages of developing one, will have way more success than one that does not. The times have changed of guys doing everything to show a lady how they feel. Confidence in a lady is one of the best characteristics that she can have. Being able to express your affection or interest in someone can strengthen your bond. Waiting on a guy to do everything can make him lose interest. And more importantly he can lose respect for your self worth." Take it from Nick; it's time to stop waiting on guys to plan dates, initiate sex, and express how they feel. Surprise him with a date, jump on him when he is least expecting it and express how important he is to you without waiting for him to start the conversation. I get it; we want guys to make us feel special. We have directly correlated his initiation of dates, sex, and expression as a sign that he truly cares about us. What's the problem with us reciprocating? Guys appreciate being taken care of just as much as we do. He can still treat you like a Queen and act chivalrously despite you taking initiative. What's a Queen without a King anyway?

Your refusal to take initiative will surely earn you a spot in a repetitive and monotonous relationship. Your lack of initiation in your relationship will also translate to other areas of your life – career progression, friendships, and personal goals. You'll be waiting for your boss to promote you instead of creating a path to promotion, you'll be waiting for your friends to call you to attend 'girl's night out' instead of planning the night and inviting them, you'll be waiting for the weight you have been wanting to lose to come off by itself instead of starting to eat healthy and beginning a workout regime, you'll be hoping that the book you've been inspired to write will write itself instead of carving out time each day to organize your thoughts, and you'll be waiting for your best self to pop up one morning instead of working hard each day to become the best version of 'you'. Take control of your life and take the role that you play in your relationship seriously. Taking initiative won't compromise how special you feel it will actually enhance it.

Chapter 23

═══════════

Your Stock Market Won't Crash

And don't let anyone tell you differently. Your stock market is your self-worth and you are definitely worth it! I know that feeling 'worth it' may seem like it shouldn't be mentioned within the realm of 'opening your legs' but it most certainty needs to be. Think back to when you first started dating and compare the guys then to those you have dated more recently. (A big difference, right? You probably even cringed at some of your earlier choices – I know I did!). As we have matured and evolved so has our taste in guys. Our self-worth has also increased; we have begun to love ourselves more and have even realized that we deserve more out of life and in relationships. Subsequently, our self-worth is directly correlated to the type of relationships that we will one day end up in.

When we have low self-esteem and minimal to no self-confidence it is much easier to be coerced into an abusive and/or manipulative relationship. We can also be coerced into staying in one where we are not fulfilled but remain in because we are complacent and are afraid of being alone, as if we will never find anyone else who loves us. When we do not think or feel that we are worth anything, how can we confidently and truthfully convey to anyone that we think or feel the opposite, let alone to the person that we share most of our intimate moments with? When we regain our control and recognize that we will no longer tolerate abuse or manipulation (or when we simply recognize that we want more out of relationships) we will invest in guys who *deserve* our time, dedication and loyalty. Our actions and how we carry ourselves say plenty about how worth it we feel.

Now I know that we all have our 'blah' moments from time-to-time where we don't feel so great about ourselves (we don't feel pretty, smart, or motivated) but do not think for one second that you deserve disrespect, being mistreated, infidelity, being talked down to, or being called outside of your name with anything other than a term of endearment. Each of us needs to whole-heartedly love ourselves and then we can welcome someone into our lives who believes we are nothing less than worth it. Our confidence is detectable; unfortunately, so is our lack of confidence.

In the same token you have to know when to walk away. Not just from the relationship but from the good sex as well. When you continuously deal with a guy that you know isn't good for you but the sex is just soooo good that you can't walk away you are settling and not honoring your worth. Do you really think that he is the only guy with a good stroke? Or who has the ability to sweat your hair out? Or that will have you pinned up against the wall like you're a 'pin the tail on the donkey'? Or who will have you driving to the store just to pick up a yellow Gatorade because your electrolytes need to be replenished after going a few rounds? Don't stay for the sex – he will have control over you every time. And know that when you stay just for that, you are subconsciously telling yourself that you don't deserve better – that you won't find better.

So yes, you are worth it and your relationships should mirror your value. This includes your friendships, family ties, and professional rapports as well. When you understand the depths of your worth you will not tolerate being around anyone who ignores your sentiments. We have to understand that if we do not feel whole there is not one pair of shoes, no amount of money, no Riesling, Moscato or Cabernet, no blue box with a necklace inside, and no passionate sex that will make us feel complete. No guy can make us feel whole and they aren't supposed to. Intimate relationships should consist of two whole people who respect each other – not two halves looking to join forces to complete one another. If you have someone who compliments your value; congratulations. If he hasn't found you yet, don't worry he's out there but just know that you are worth it! Your stock market will never crash!

Chapter 24

Courtship Hasn't Sunk

You haven't boarded the ship yet. Chivalry may seem like a thing of the past but it is only because you have individually allowed it to be. The idea of chivalry has collectively changed from what I can see; it has become less about a guy being a gentleman and more about what he can do for you – how many free dinners you can get out of the deal. Let's be real, the majority of us have gone on at least one date with someone we weren't all that interested in because "hey, can't turn down a free meal." But chivalry is much more than a free meal, having the door opened and our seats pulled out before we sit down. Courting is about a guy showing us that he is a gentleman: courteous, respectful, courageous, a provider and protector.

If our only perception of chivalry consists of being taken out on three dates before giving up the cookies then it is our fault why 'chivalry is dead'. You can't define chivalry as a guy taking you out to dinner and buying you cute gifts that you can show off to your good friends and to the "friends" that you don't really know all that well on social media and then call him 'emotionally unavailable' once you catch feelings after giving it up. He was always emotionally unavailable but you never required him to be anything other than an ATM for you or an accessory to show off to your friends. Going back to standards, if you require any guy that you are investing time in to be a gentleman then chivalry would not seem like such a foreign concept. And to the ladies who are still trapped in the 'Independent Woman' era – it's time to resurface back to reality! Being able to provide for and take care of yourself is admirable (and I believe necessary) but guys like to feel needed. If he feels that you don't need him because you are so independent why would he stick around? Why would he spend his hard earned money to take you out if you keep throwing it in his face that you can afford to pay for your own meal? Why would he exert his energy to show you how much he appreciates spending time with you if you keep throwing in his face how much you can do for yourself? Why do you have to prove that you are strong enough to open the jar of pickles – let him open it! And why would he grab a ladder to reach for your cookies if you keep throwing it in his face that your cookies are so high up on the shelf that he wouldn't be able reach them with three ladders?

It is up to each of us to revive chivalry: to stop giving up the cookies before truly getting to know the guy we are dealing with. Allow a guy to show you that he is capable of being a gentleman for the long term. Allow a guy to show you that he is respectable and fascinating enough to introduce to your friends and maybe eventually your family. Allow a guy to wear the pants; if he's really a gentleman he will let you pick them out. Allow yourself to treat him how you would like him to treat you. And allow yourself to embrace being courted – it is less about what he can do for you and more about what you are worth.

Chapter 25

No Need For A Timesheet

This job doesn't require you to record your vacation and sick time. You won't even need to sign up for a 401(k) or keep track of all the tasks that you performed throughout the year for your end of the year evaluation. Your promotion falls into your lap and whether you would like more responsibility is sometimes dictated by life. Nonetheless being in a relationship is absolutely a full-time job that requires your full attention. The fun element of the job is that you and the guy you are dating have the ability to customize your job descriptions and no one in Human Resources needs to approve them. And since no one in HR needs to approve your job description, when your relationship goes through rocky times please do not complain to HR (the peanut gallery) about how you don't need a man.

If you are not ready to add another full-time job to your resume then being single may prove to be a better option for you. If you feel as though a part-time relationship would work best with the amount of free time that you have, that would of course need to be discussed with whomever you are looking to engage in a relationship with but just know that you will not reap full-time benefits. I know that some of you are like, "well at my job if you work 20 hours a week you receive full-time benefits." This is true but the Fair Labor Standards Act (FLSA) does not regulate relationships; good try!

My friend Imani always bails when relationships require her full attention. She loves the beginning stages of getting to know a guy – the dinners, the constant texting back and forth, the giddiness, the late nights and early mornings, the flirting, the butterflies, having control of dangling the cookie. But as soon as that honeymoon stage fades and it's time to take the relationship to the next level she suddenly looses interest. Imani either doesn't realize or doesn't care that relationships are a full-time job. I even think that it's selfish of her to lead a guy on and then run when she has to put work in. Since the majority of us work a full-time job because we have bills to pay and want to ultimately create comfortable lives for ourselves, any other full-time job that we welcome into our lives should be voluntary. The voluntary welcome should eliminate playing games like Imani does. If you are not willing to put the full-time work in then just be honest and don't string anyone along in the process.

Chapter 26

Imbalanced Milky Way

That's the way it has been and the way it will continue to be. Same galaxy, two different planets and oh what a difference a planet makes. We are absolutely wired differently than guys and as long as we are aware of the differences then our relationships with them should have less frustration. Below is a list that my good friend Ron and I have compiled that outline *some* of what we believe ladies need to understand:

- He does not like to be blamed for cheating on you just because you had a dream that he did

- Don't expect him to telepathically know exactly what you need and want, regardless of how long you've been together

- Three hour conversations on the phone should

stay between you and your best friends – talking all of the time is what we like to do

- You can't have a guy with old-fashioned values and still want to be a new era 'independent woman' – something has to give
- Guys mature later than we do, be prepared to deal with some immaturity
- At the same time, his age won't automatically determine his level of maturity
- There's no such thing as a "bad boy gentleman" so stop looking for him
- There's nothing wrong with dating a respectable guy
- Don't hold what is bothering you in, communicate to him what's on your mind
- It's not what you say, it's how you say it
- Guys love to be nurtured (and when you cook for them)
- Sex gets old, what else are you bringing to the table?
- Have standards not blind expectations
- He thinks your intelligence is sexy – don't be afraid to show it

- Judge how respectable he is by his actions, not by how long you make him wait for cookies; just because you're making him wait doesn't mean someone else is

And the one thing that guys need to know about us is that no matter how much they try to ration in their heads they will never understand our need to have so many shoes!

I won't go into the psychological and biological differences between the two genders but wanted you to think twice about getting mad at him when he doesn't want to:

- Talk, talk, talk, talk, talk
- Go shopping with you all day
- Pay for dinners after you've been dating for a while (especially when you started expecting it)
- Talk, talk, talk, talk, talk some more
- Spend all day everyday with you

Or when he:

- Inappropriately mentions something at the most inopportune time

- Doesn't text you back in 3.4 seconds, one minute, five minutes, or even an hour after you hit send
- Is slightly insensitive every month (he will never fully understand what it feels like to be bloated, have cramps, eat insane amounts of food for no reason, and have uncontrollable mood swings)
- Occasionally acts immaturely
- Wants you to give him more of your attention
- Is at an age where you think he should carry himself with a certain level of poise and sensibleness but he sometimes acts the opposite
- Doesn't think twice about putting the toilet seat down (for you couples living together)

Although I think that as humans we are all more alike than we are not it's no secret that we communicate and react to situations differently than guys. Before getting angry with him for not doing something he isn't wired to do or understand – just take a deep breath...it's an imbalanced milky way.

Chapter 27

Delayed Fourth of July

Because sparks can take time to ignite. I know that we have been sold the dream of fireworks, sunsets, and long walks on the beach but there are times where the fireworks won't go off, the sun won't set, and the beach has more rocks and shells than sand. If you really like him but the energy between you two seems to be a bit off, work on it. If having sex with him has been embarrassingly awkward, talk through it. If your personalities clash at times but you enjoy his company, stick it out. "Hard work pays off" applies to relationships as well – fireworks don't always happen in July.

I remember when my friend Taylor started dating her boyfriend several years ago. They had sexual chemistry (or maybe that's all they wanted to explore at the time) and that's about it. Initially they seemed like an unlikely couple but after some time went by they enjoyed each other's company so much so that they officially started dating. What I learned from Taylor's relationship is that the guy who may be the best candidate may not be packaged in the wrapping paper that we are looking for. He may not be dressed in the clothes that we find the most fashionable. He may not listen to the same music as we do. He may not be of the same build that we are normally attracted to. And he definitely will not be Ken but he will be worth it.

Opposites do attract and because of this we should be careful about who we are dismissing at first sight. Again, looks aren't everything so don't let your eyes make a decision for you. *Hear* what he has to say, *touch* his humor, *see* what he is about, *taste* his intellect, and *look* for his potential. Trust your senses! Don't become skeptical if fireworks aren't shooting off into the sky as soon as you would like them to. Or maybe they fizzled soon before you'd hoped but that's okay; you can always relight them because fireworks don't always happen in July. Let's be realistic; if you determine your level of chemistry with someone by the amount of explosives that goes off then you may be doomed from the start. There are so many other gauges that can be used to determine if he is worth investing more time in: does he make you laugh? Is he a gentleman? Does he have the same standards as you? Is he knowledgeable or resourceful? Is he goal-oriented? Does his presence comfort you? I'm not saying that you should give up on your vision of fireworks, sunsets, and long walks on the beach but just know that they may not be handed to you. "Hard work pays off" applies to relationships as well.

Chapter 28

─────────

Oil Change, Air Filter, Tune Up

Jiffy Lube won't be able to assist you. You will need to look under the hood on your own. Every guy that you meet will need an oil change, new air filter, and tune up. This does not suggest that anything is wrong with him, it just means that so many other factors have shaped his ideals about relationships and how to treat a lady as I briefly mentioned in Chapter 10. You not only have to teach him how to treat you but how to love and nurture you as well. We don't come with "how-to" manuals so don't expect him to automatically know "how-to". Even the guy who has accumulated a lot of mileage will need some fine-tuning. The guy who has eaten a lot of cookies will need to take direction in order to get it right – just the way you like. The guy who has sisters will still need a refresher.

The only tool that you need for prying open and taking a look underneath the hood is patience. Just like service on a car, maintenance is required every so often so do not get frustrated when the time comes. And you will need service as well! Show attentiveness to your "rust" and openness to his suggestions. You shouldn't be discouraged at your needing periodic service or that you will have to look under his hood because well-maintained vehicles (relationships) last longer. Let's not forget that no matter what level our relationship sits on we are all human. **We all:**

- make mistakes
- will never get it right all of the time
- say hurtful things with pure intentions
- will be on the receiving end of being hurt at some point
- have insecurities
- fear being alone
- want to be happy
- want to be loved

Tune-ups are a necessity for growth so be kind. I'll forewarn you about acting the way my friend Bria did when she realized that her boyfriend needed a tune-up. He hadn't been in a long-term relationship for a number of years so his communication and compromising skills were not as polished as Bria would have liked. Instead of exercising patience she would start "debates" (arguments) with him and constantly remind him of how much of a bad communicator he was. She would tell him how he needed to compromise more and that in order for a relationship to work two people needed to be committed on all fronts. I agree with her last point but I think that Bria was doing what a lot of us have learned how to do – *talk but not teach*. Instead of using her energy to help him become a better communicator she nagged him about it. Instead of using her time to help him with compromising she would become frustrated at his stubbornness. If Bria showed a little more understanding, compassion, and patience within her relationship, it wouldn't have become as stressful as it did. Because of the way she handled her boyfriend I'd even say that Bria was way overdue for an oil change, air filter, and tune-up – maybe even a few spark plug replacements too!

Section V:
When You're In A Serious Relationship

Chapter 29

Benjamin Franklin

Your relationship won't work if you don't. Give 100 percent or don't give any at all! I tend to think that if we put 100 percent into any of our endeavors we will always see a return on our time, energy, and dedication; even if the return is that we simply gained knowledge that we didn't have before. I was having a conversation about relationships with a good friend of mine recently and he opened up about what makes his relationship of almost ten years so solid:

When my woman tells me I am creative, insightful or that she loves my artistic views and aspirations, this not only pleases me but it creates more of an increased ambition than I once needed. To me, the unconditional support from a partner is far more than a "backing" or an "agreement"; it's when they communicate with each other by simply understanding and respecting ones thoughts, feelings and opinions. In my past experiences, whenever I felt a female was unsupportive or didn't seem encouraging, I certainly wouldn't expand the relationship any more than friendship and/or casual sex. Today, I can honestly say that I am grateful and pleased within my relationship. The reason for this is that together we have communicated positively, laughed hysterically, cried emotionally and grown together spiritually. Without an open-minded, caring, supportive woman, I may not have found the desire to open my heart to someone nor achieve my goals." – Timothy Davis

As Tim alluded to, giving 100 percent doesn't always

translate from action but from encouraging words as well. It is invaluable when you can genuinely uplift, inspire, and show appreciation of your significant other. Being in a relationship is a selfless act and it is not just about your needs and wants. It takes 100 percent selflessness plus 100 percent compromise plus 100 percent communication plus 100 percent support plus 100 percent trust plus 100 percent forgiveness plus 100 percent nurture plus 100 percent patience plus 100 percent negotiation plus 100 percent encouragement plus 100 percent dedication plus 100 percent honesty (minus the genuine white lies that we all tell in order to avoid hurting each other's feelings). If this sounds like too much then you are not ready to be in a committed relationship and that is totally fine. The more you put into a relationship the more that you will get out of it. *Your relationship won't work if you don't.* Give 100 percent or don't give any at all!

Chapter 30

═══════════

LOVE You > Him

It is absolutely necessary! Just because you are putting 100 percent effort into a relationship does not mean that you need to love him more than you love yourself. Here are some words of advice from my good friend Rachel: "It's important to love yourself before loving someone else because you need to know who you are before you can truly open up to someone. If you can have a relationship with yourself and are content being alone then you can begin to appreciate someone else for all the reasons they are like you, but even more for all the reasons they are different. Typically, I think we attract people who are a reflection of us in some way but how can you be aware of this connection without discovering every aspect of yourself first? Once you are aware of your traits, strengths and weaknesses you can find someone to compliment the positive and possibly overcome the negative. Allowing someone to come into your life and help you grow as a person is one of the best things about love. Know yourself and be confident in who you are so that you and your partner can then grow together and develop new traits, new hobbies; without losing yourself in the process."

...*without losing yourself in the process*. Being in a relationship is not about becoming so infatuated with the other person that you lose sight of your ambitions, interests, passion, or happiness. When someone is right for you they will enhance all of those aspects of your life plus more (and your energy and attitude should enhance their life as well). I have seen a lot of ladies become severely heartbroken after a breakup but not due to the actual breakup, more because she loved him more than she loved herself – huge mistake. Loving him more than you love yourself can be very dangerous as every one of his needs and wants will supersede yours. His energy will trump yours, his attitude will control your mood, and his moves will dictate the direction you move towards. Even though love is selfless I mentioned earlier that intimate relationships should consist of two whole beings coming together not two halves looking to complete one another. As Rachel pointed out, the love you have for yourself should never waver because you are in a relationship; it should grow in fact. Don't confuse being selfless with putting your needs on the backburner or dismissing your thoughts and emotions. Selflessness is an act in which we can demonstrate our understanding that the world does not revolve around us – that we can put someone else's needs and interests ahead of ours in a given situation. So practice selflessness but love yourself more.

Chapter 31

Listen → Input → Repeat

Communication is the most important component in a relationship, so much so that my good friend Theo is going to take over this chapter. "Everyone wants that ideal relationship where you can finish each other's sentences. We all want to be understood so well that we don't need to fully explain ourselves to the people that we are with. They just "get" us. But the truth of the matter is that it takes time to establish. *Time and understanding.* The difficulties that we face in our relationships that keep us at bay from this ideal manner of spiritual language lies in our obvious difference. Guys and ladies communicate differently. Guys are so direct and straightforward, whereas ladies either don't say anything, or don't directly say what it is they want. Ladies want a guy to make that extra effort into really understanding her. In this self-created and issued test of endurance, ladies tend to make a large mistake. They will associate a guy's desire to have her based on the results of her self issued test. Ladies let me stop you in your tracks right now. Your test is flawed. If a guy wants you he'll show it when you are around and when you are not around. I don't mean to burst your bubble but we don't have to go through the same experiences in the world. The smallest effort he placed into you, just to make you smile, might've taken some extreme measures.

A lady commits her emotions to a guy in such an extreme measure that she can both love him and hate him to the same extremes. Our truest intentions are based in our actions. You love him and your actions, in their entirety, show it. I'm telling you to look at his actions in their entirety. Just because he doesn't do exactly what you want or tend to your areas of discomfort doesn't mean that he does not want to be with you. If anything, because he wants you he'll never stop trying. What you haven't noticed is that your unhappiness bothers him. And unfortunately making ladies happy isn't' as simple as 'act and repeat'. So there is a learning curve associated. He has to learn you and because he wants you he'll learn every inch of you. Guys aren't great listeners but we are damn good observers. We are natural DNA encoded hunters. Your guy will notice how you flip your hair or your slightest facial expression because how you feel matters to him. Ladies just have so many feelings that oftentimes guys find themselves quite overloaded in tending to every single nook and cranny of ladies' emotions. So calm down and relax. He wants you.

The secret way that we communicate is in our vulnerabilities. You have to understand that guys grew up in a society where we never felt protected. The general consensus is that we are guys so we have to "man up" and tackle adversity a, b, and c, regardless of whether or not we are 'man enough' to face them. When a guy entrusts you with his vulnerabilities you are good with him. You get what you want out of him by approaching him correctly. Don't complain all the time or nag him. That's too annoying; he'll shut out your voice completely. Sit down with him and talk. But before you talk, open him up to listening. Think about it. We all want to be understood. No guy wants to come to see you, in hopes of getting away from the world, only to walk into a conversation about what he doesn't do or how inconsiderate he is. Ask him how his day was. Ask him how his family is doing. How is he feeling about himself? What items in his life are challenging him? We currently live in a world where manliness has been filtered and attacked. Even football isn't the same. Listen to him and he'll listen to you.

The integrity of communication is maintained through honesty and openness. Never lie to a guy you want or a guy you are with – trust me. If you do, he'll instinctively register you as being like the rest of the world and you'll knock yourself out of significance. Guys have almost been trained to walk on eggshells when talking to ladies. That makes it difficult to just open up. We talk to our friends with no sense of restraint. It's one of the beauties of having great friendships; people can just be themselves. *Let him be himself.*

Lastly I have to touch on a dangerous element of communication between us; something that I call, "The Challenge". Ladies have a way of naturally challenging a guy. She'll argue with him for no reason. She may play games to make him jealous, whatever. Never, and I mean NEVER emasculate him. There is a difference between challenging someone and disrespecting them. If you disrespect him, you burn the bridge of communication with him. He won't want to talk to you and he won't want to be around you. Guys catch a bad rap and get butchered all the time for the smallest things. There are so many conversations of deadbeat dads, guys in prison, more ladies in college, ladies making more money, guys not being "men", etcetera. I'm all for ladies coming up in the world but the bashing of guys takes it to an all time high. Even lesbians bash guys lol. Uplift the guy you want and support him. Make him feel more like a 'man' in a place where his manhood is constantly attacked.

A relationship is about how we connect as a couple but it is also about us as individuals. I can't love you if I'm broken and messed up internally.

Communication isn't simply rooted in us. My intentions and considerations have to be rooted in you. And yours have to be rooted in me. That is how we speak without words being said. That is how we can finish the other's sentences. The fluidity of how we speak has nothing to do with a title, a game, our friends, or our past experiences. We speak based on the depth of our connection. Myself in you and you in me."

Chapter 32

Perpetual Stimulus

Intellectually.   *Emotionally.*   *Physically.*
Continuously stimulating him on these three levels is extremely important. Most of us grew up with the notion that "all guys want to do is get in your pants" – while I'm not denying that he wants to get in your pants, believe it or not he has other needs. Although guys tend not to show as much emotion as we'd like sometimes, my friend Ron outlined a few pieces of information that can help us bond with him (the guy we are dating not Ron) emotionally:

- If a guy was spoiled by his mom growing up, no matter how old he gets he will forever in his heart be a "mama's boy"
  - Don't get frustrated with him, talk through his expectations and

understand that he will require extra
nurture

- Guys love when we are open-minded instead of
closed-off and uptight
    - We can get so accustomed to saying "no"
    that it closes us off from fully bonding
    with the guy we are with – say yes to
    trying something new
- Talking about and being knowledgeable about
sports is a turn-on
    - It's true that not all guys like sports but
    take the time to become somewhat fluent
    in an area or with a topic in which he is
    interested in, you'd be surprised by how
    much it means to him
- Allow him to teach you
    - Guys like to feel needed, don't be shy
    about letting him teach you – open
    yourself up to learn from him
- Complacency and not compromising is a major
turn off
    - Perpetual stimulus. Even though some
    guys may enjoy routine, it doesn't

translate well when it comes to relationships. Don't allow your relationship to become monotonous and don't act so stubbornly

- Guys are scared of being rejected
  - o Even the most macho guy can get nervous when it comes to approaching a lady. Don't think that he is so 'tough' that he should be able to easily approach a situation or conversation that you've been wanting to have – guys get nervous and intimidated too

There are multiple ways in which we can perpetually stimulate the guy we are with but I have a feeling that we haven't been thinking outside of the box enough. Spend more time getting to know him instead of ridiculing him about the flaws that he is already aware of. No one is perfect, remember? He wants to be intellectually, emotionally, and physically stimulated by you; don't deprive him!

Chapter 33

Two Cars On The Road

Stop acting like a Princess! I know that the majority of us grew up thinking that all we needed was a glass slipper in order for our fairy tale life to commence. Maybe Aladdin would take us on the ride of our lives on his "magic carpet" or maybe all we had to do was kiss a frog. If you want to experience Disney then book a flight to Florida or California[3]. This is not to say that your relationship won't have any magical moments but come down to earth with me for a second; relationships are not like the fantasies that we grew up watching and idolizing. I mentioned earlier that we should only invest our time in guys who recognize that we are nothing less than a Queen – I stand firm on that belief. But we also

---

[3] There are international locations as well if you are interested.

have to treat him like a King; pampering and catering is a two-way street.

I know a few ladies who think catering to a guy is being subservient but being catered to is a necessity. I haven't decided yet if they are narcissistic, misguided, lazy, or a combination of all three. If you want flowers, a new pair of shoes, your nails or hair done, chocolate during that time of a month, a new purse, fancy dinners, sexual favors, surprise romantic outings, for him to watch your favorite TV lineup with you, and passionate trips on his "magical carpet" then you'd better get your creative juices flowing. It would be easy for me to tell you to give him a blow job whenever he wants (don't giggle, we are all adults here) because that's the male equivalent to flowers but the truth is that guys enjoy being pampered and catered to just as much as we do. And of course he genuinely and graciously appreciates BJ's as well.

There is no one size fits all guide to catering to your guy but if he goes out of his way to make you feel special do not hesitate to reciprocate. Pay attention to what he likes or what he mentions to you about his day – stay alert for opportunities. Does he work on his feet for most of the day? Massage his feet every once in a while. I don't want to hear that it's disgusting because you have no problem with getting a pedicure and having someone else touching your dirty feet (yup, I said it!). I also don't want to hear that guy's feet are "dirtier" or "smellier" or "crustier" than yours are – feet are feet are feet. Fine, you don't want to massage his feet but what else can you do to make him feel special? Does he have a favorite sports team? Does he have a favorite brand of shoes, ties, shirts, watches, or cologne? Can you make sure that you have his favorite drink and/or snack at your place for when he comes over? Has he been raving about tickets that he has wanted to purchase? Can you purchase the tickets for him or contribute to the amount if they are too expensive? Does he love when you wear a certain dress, shoe, or perfume? Has he been asking you to accompany him on an outdoors trip but you hate bugs? Pack up some bug spray, bring a sweatshirt and finally agree to his trip.

Creativity may not be your strong point but I promise that all you have to do is pay attention and stay attentive. When you are out shopping you somehow always see outfits that would look nice on your best friends, right? Or when you find a trinket that your favorite coworker "absolutely would love to have" you get it, right? You already have it in you just translate it to your relationship. To keep it completely honest I must add that if you do not pamper or cater to him he will definitely find someone else who does. Communicate with one another and even ask him how he likes to be pampered if you have to. And if he is the type to take your pampering for granted (he's looking for more than one lady to cater to him) well, I hope that you know what you should do with him!

Chapter 34

Listen To His Moves

Because actions will forever speak louder than words. Start paying attention to the things that he is not saying and you will learn a tremendous amount about him. Look for patterns: inconsistencies vs. consistencies. The patterns that you are looking for are not just to uncover the negative (e.g. cheating) but for positive opportunities as well. If you see that his pattern includes working out a few times a week you can give him a coupon for a free 30-minute massage that you will be administering (combining your thoughtfulness and creativity). If you see that his pattern includes listening to a particular musician or reading a particular author's books, look out for upcoming material from the artist to purchase for him and/or purchase a classic piece of work by the artist for his collection. If you recognize that he has been feeling unappreciated, you can handwrite in a card for him expressing how much you appreciate him being in your life – guys love feeling appreciated by their lady. It can be so simple – the more you watch the more you will learn without having to ask questions.

I asked my good friend Azaria to weight in: "Time will show you how sincere he is about all the wonderful things he has been saying. It's a great predictor. It gives you the opportunity to see the consistencies or inconsistencies of his behavior. Keeping it 100, we all are inconsistent at times so don't think that because he stops calling for a day here and there that something is wrong. He may even have to reschedule a date or two. It may be that work, school or other priorities have monopolized his time for the moment. But depending on the level of the relationship, you may want to check in with him to see if he needs your assistance or that coupon for a 30-minute massage. Show him that you care and have appreciated the consistency in his actions (communication). Allowing time also helps both of you to gain personal investments in the relationship.

If you believe that guys work harder when they haven't tasted the cookies, allowing time and the development of personal investments can pay off. He still may not outright express his undying feelings for you like your favorite romance movie but you will have substance and actions over a period of time for you to know that he in fact cares about you, your welfare and needs."

As cliché as it sounds time will truly reveal the truth. But as Azaria said, don't give up on him or get mad at the first sign of inconsistency because it's true that we are all inconsistent at times. Do you consistently keep in touch with *everyone* that you care about? NO! I think that the majority of us do our best to keep in touch with the people that we care about but life happens and sometimes it happens fast. We all get a little off course and sidetracked at times. I also understand that guys go after what they want but at the same time they are human – we are creatures of habits and complacency; hence the reason why relationships are a full-time job, they require both people working hard together. So practice more patience and learn to take mental notes of his patterns. Don't be afraid to jump in when you see an opportunity or jump back when you see a red flag. Cut him some slack just as you would like him to cut some for you. Pay attention!

Chapter 35

─────────

Camaraderie

Friends, pals, buddies, besties, BFFs! Having a solid friendship with him may be what can ultimately save your relationship during rocky times. The friendship won't signify that you will know everything about him, rather that you have a basic understanding and appreciation for who he is and what he has to offer the world. Sometimes love can't even save a friendship but 'like' can. Love can fade and wither away but when you genuinely like someone (their company, personality, quirks) it holds a lot of weight. There is no need for you to rush into a serious relationship because it will fail if you do not have a strong foundation from the beginning. Instead, work on becoming the best of friends first. Developing a friendship will also let you know if you want to pursue an intimate relationship later on. Too many of us rush into relationships never fully understanding who we are dealing with. We listen less and talk more, observe less and talk more, and understand less and talk more.

Building a friendship with a guy you may be more seriously interested in down the road is no different than building a platonic relationship with one of your girlfriends. With your girlfriends you venture out together, build trust, honor respect, laugh, share goals, vent, disagree, forgive, laugh some more, and genuinely get to know one another. Without developing a friendship before jumping into a relationship your success rate will be abysmal. I have a friend; I'll call her Zoe, who used to date a guy named Ian. Zoe and Ian became really good friends before they even considered exploring the idea of intimately dating. After two years of dating they decided to call it quits but still have a great friendship to this day. I believe that there is no way that after a rocky two years of dating Ian and Zoe would have continued speaking to one another if it weren't for the fact that they had a strong friendship beforehand.

In the moments where you feel like he's on your last nerve think about how great of a friendship you have with him. Some of you just rolled your eyes and that's okay. If you want your thoughts in that moment to only be consumed with how frustrating he is instead of trying to think back to more positive times then that's okay too. So as long as you don't forget that your friendship adds a unique dimension of strength to your relationship. Those memories are always available for you to tap into. When one of your girlfriends is getting on your last nerve you always get to a point where you assess not only what she did or said but how much you cherish her friendship; that combination most likely determined how understanding and empathic you wanted to be towards her. The same can reign true to your intimate affairs. Treat him how you would treat your best friend!

Chapter 36

Exit Left Off Stage

No drama please! There aren't many things that I find less attractive than a drama filled relationship. The excessive arguing, cat and mouse nitpicking, pulling innocent outsiders into the drama web, constant gossip, unattended insecurities, the blame game – the list goes on. If you enjoy drama so much so that you cannot live without it at least be ambitious; sign up for acting lessons and aim towards starring in a Broadway show. Or simply catch up on "reality" TV episodes but leave it out of your relationship. We all love a little guilty pleasure drama from time-to-time but we also need to be able to turn it off in order to function. Your relationship will never prosper as long as drama is at the forefront because you will be stifled and going in continuous circles – having the same arguments, the same conversations, and the same difficulties. If you believe that adding and/or keeping drama in your relationship keeps things 'interesting' you are right but oh so wrong at the same time. There are far more positive additions that can be added to your relationship in order to keep it 'interesting'.

There are some guys who love drama too – avoid them! You will be so thankful that you saved yourself from all of the extra commotion. Someone who is so immersed in drama and what other people are doing will not contribute to your growth; they will be nothing more than a hindrance, a distraction. If you are in need of a distraction then you can listen to some music until you drift off, log onto Facebook, take a walk, play a game, explore your creative abilities, log onto Facebook, watch TV, go shopping, read a book, or log onto Facebook. There are far more mechanisms that you can use as a distraction than being dramatic.

If you find comfort in dramatic situations then the dating scene would greatly appreciate it if you did not spread the wealth. Striving to keep your relationship balanced, healthy, and exciting all the while trying to remain positive in a society filled with negativity requires a lot of energy; the remaining energy need not be spent on combating drama in a space that should be comfortable. We should spend more time working out the details in our own intimate affairs instead of obsessing over what other couples are doing. If you are more intrigued by Jay-Z and Beyonce's latest travel spots, Robert Pattinson and Kristen Stewart getting back together, Kanye and Kim's engagement, and/or Brad and Angelina's next move than your own relationship then there is a huge problem! Your intimate affairs need T.L.C not D.R.A.M.A.

Chapter 37

Elegance X Erotic

A.k.a lady in the streets plus freak in the sheets! On the sheets, in the kitchen, on the couch, in the shower, on the table – whatever you prefer but you get the point. I think I can speak for all guys when I say that they love when a lady has class (when she can accompany him to his work event or meet his friends and family) and when she can trade in the fancy outfit to do that little thing he likes. Loosen up a little bit and let your hair down. Explore your inner freak and keep things exciting. Obviously there are components of the sexual arena that we are not willing to experience or maybe we have a to-do list that only our husbands will be able to check off – if this is true then it is up to us to draw those boundaries. It is also up to us to stay open-minded and aware of ways in which we can feed our sexual appetite.

Realistically, sex is not the most important aspect in a relationship although it is a form of communication and expression. Even though I view sex as being natural somewhere along the way it has become a taboo subject. Not to mention the annoying double standards that we face when it comes to amounts of sexual partners in our repertoire. If we are more open and communicative about sex (beyond the physical act), I think some of our frustrations will die down. For example, we accuse guys of being sex-a-holics; "all they do is think about sex" but we talk about it just as much as they do if not more.

We think about it, dream about it, and sometimes even share the intimate details of our encounters with our really close friends: A guy may say to his friend, "Yea, I hit that! Yup, from the back too bro!" and that's the end of that. A lady, on the other hand, may say to her friend, "Girrrrrrrrrrrllll! Mmmm, it was so crazy. So I finally decided to wear those purple panties with the lace and polka dots; you know the ones we picked out at the mall that time? Yea, those! When he got here I had some Vanilla candles lit to set the mood. We were sitting on the couch for like 40 minutes just talking – nothing super serious. Then, OMG we started kissing and ended up doing it right on the couch girl. You know the couch I'm talking about? The brown leather one with the end table from IKEA right next to it..."

What's the issue with opening up about our sexual desires or frustrations with the guy we are intimately involved with? Sex is not taboo and if you disagree, it's time to have a stern talk with your parents to discuss why they participated in such a horrid act that has ultimately allowed you to experience the wonders of life. We have been fed so many 'Scarlet letter' worthy tales about how bad sex is for us (or how bad having sex out of wedlock is). While we all have the right to our beliefs my suggestion is that if we are vulnerable enough to engage sexually with someone, we should be vulnerable enough to have honest conversations about our sexual feelings, desires, and appetite.

According to ABC, "Pornography has grown into a $10 billion business — bigger than the NFL, the NBA and Major League Baseball combined — and some of the nation's best-known corporations are quietly sharing the profits."[4] This tells me that many people are vicariously living out their fantasies or desires by watching other people in action. These same people are probably too embarrassed to admit that they enjoy watching pornography to either quiet their sexual thoughts or fulfill their sexual appetite because of the fear of being judged or pinned with a 'Scarlett letter'. There are obviously those who watch porn for what they'd consider "fun" and those who can be labeled "sick in the head" because of their obsession and/or wanting to view young children. I am not at all making a case for watching pornography, just that numbers don't lie. How can a $10 billion business grow to such if barely anyone supports it? I don't have a remedy for pornography nor am I trying to conjure up one. I do think that if we draw our boundaries, are more open about sex, and are not so ashamed of it like we have been coerced into believing we should be then our intimate affairs would benefit greatly. Don't be ashamed or punish yourself for thinking about the very act that has allowed you take your first breath.

---

[4] http://abcnews.go.com/Primetime/story?id=132001

Chapter 38

Strategic Battlefields

Pick your battles but leave your camouflage, ammunition, eye black and victory flag on your home base! Disagreements naturally occur within any healthy relationship but they do not have to dominate. Most of us are more concerned with getting our points across, getting the last word, and winning an argument than we are with trying to come to an amicable agreement. We don't need to be more forceful; we need to be more strategic. Every battle is not one that we need to gear up for. It's okay to let some things slide and create a mental note. If we approach disagreements with the intention of 'understanding, solving, and compromising' instead of "la la la la I'm not listening because you're wrong and I'm always right" then our frustrations will be lessened and our relationship less strained. This goes with saying that you should address anything that is bothering you as long as you do so with the intent of understanding, solving, and compromising. There is a major difference between approaching him and aggressively talking at or down to him/attacking his character and talking gently *to* him with the intention of resolving an unsettled issue.

I feel that some of us are so concerned with "getting played" that we don't want him to think he can sneak anything by us, thus creating part of the reason we struggle with picking our battles. I also feel that some of us have severe control issues that hinder us from strategically engaging in a dispute. But most strongly I feel that some of us have the hugest chip on our shoulder that stifles not just our ability to maturely survive a disagreement but to holistically grow. I'm not sure if the chip on our shoulder stems from the subconscious need to prove that we can 'compete' with guys now that we have more opportunities, if it's a learned behavior, or if passing up an argument doesn't seem appealing. Either way, strategically picking battles will shift our attention in our relationship and increase our relationship productivity. There's no need to have gloves on at all times!

Think about how many battles you'd be fighting in if you addressed everything that he did or said that annoyed you? And think about how many battles he'd be initiating if he confronted you every time that you did or said something that annoyed him. Relationships don't have to become an active battlefield just a strategic one. Before you engage in a heated disagreement think about its relevance in the grand scheme of your relationship. Will your relationship be better off if you let "it" slide? If you don't address "it" will it spiral into larger more complicated issues down the road? Think before you lash out and leave your camouflage, ammunition, eye black and victory flag on your home base!

Chapter 39

Don't Wait To Exhale

Like Whitney, Angela, Loretta, and Lela; woooooooooossssssssssaaaaaaaaaaaaaaah! Just relax – dating is supposed to be fun! Yes it takes a lot of work, patience, time, dedication, forgiveness, communication, creativity and you opening your mind but it is all worth it. Be sure that you don't overthink your relationships though; I know, "you're the one who told us to open our minds in the first place!" I did and I am staying true to its importance although in the same breath overthinking will cause you nothing but stress. If your dating scene is buried in negativity, anxiety, uncertainty, drama, and overcast clouds then it is time for a change of scenery. Every relationship has its ups and downs but you should never compromise your happiness throughout it all. There's no need to get crazy – have fun, stay open-minded, be vulnerable, learn as much as you can and don't wait to exhale. Know what you want and don't be afraid of going after it. Know who you are dealing with and never dismiss your intuition. Know that there is more power in your thoughts than your looks.

Don't think that letting a guy take charge will compromise your independence and cause you to become submissive. Don't think that picking your battles will compromise your voice. Don't think that being single will compromise your worth. Don't think that giving up the cookies 'too soon' will compromise his respect for you. Don't think that holding out on that snickerdoodle 'long enough' will automatically make him respect you. Don't think that stopping the cycle will compromise your moral conscience. Don't be afraid to embrace a good guy. Don't be afraid to wait. Don't be afraid to exhale. Don't be afraid to walk away. Don't be afraid to cater to him. Don't be self-conscious about being catered to – you deserve it! Don't be afraid of having your heart broken. Don't be afraid of 'the single life'. Don't be afraid of falling in love. As my good friend Megan said, don't be someone who "...falls in love with potential instead of actions. Potential can easily pollute your decision making."

Intimacy far exceeds the realm of sex. We have to do a better job at being vulnerable with our clothes on – pillow talking without the pillows – allowing ourselves to be naked before we undress – requiring that our mind be given the first orgasm. There is no need to rush into a relationship for the sake of being in a relationship – get to know yourself and allow relationships to organically take their course. Set your standards and never allow any outside forces to convince you of lowering or raising them. Make yourself a promise:

No more searching!

No more chasing!

No more continuing the cycle!

No more desperation!

No more nagging!

No more lying to myself!

No more assuming!

No more settling!

No more excessive baggage!

No more ignoring red flags!

No more searching for Ken!

No more purple panties with lace! Just joking!

Don't complicate your love life. Don't run from vulnerability. Don't skip out on taking the initiative. Keep the peanut gallery out of your relationship; they will make you second-guess yourself. Tap into your intuition when you need clarity. *Hear* what he has to say, *touch* his humor, *see* what he is about, *taste* his intellect, and *look* for his potential. Trust your senses! Never lose sight of who you are and never become so absorbed in him that you lose yourself. Never love him more than you love yourself. Keep your mind sexy – open your mind before you open your legs!

Bonus Chapter: The Friend Zone

Ladies! Ladies! Ladies! Ladies!!! Before I get into why we have to stop putting guys in the friend zone let me first delve into the history. I believe that the friend zone was a term initially created by guys who weren't getting any play from the women that they really wanted. Therefore in the guy's mind if she wasn't sleeping with him then she clearly considered him to be a friend. Women have since taken the term friend zone and found a way to use it to their advantage – as a way to not be upfront and honest about how they truly feel. I think it's important to note where the misunderstanding lies within our first interaction.

Before a guy approaches a lady he has already outlined what he is going to say, placed her into a category and he obviously knows that he is sexually attracted to her or else he wouldn't be wasting his time. A lady, on the other hand, can be completely content with having a guy friend because we are emotional creatures – when a guy approaches we may not be thinking about sex right off the bat; unless he is just too fine! The miscommunication regarding the friend zone stems from that first interaction. If a lady understands that a guy is only approaching because he is sexually attracted to her then she may think twice about leading him on: giving out her number, agreeing to call, flirting with him, etc. If a guy understands that a lady may only be flirting back with him because she doesn't want to be rude then maybe he will think twice about being subtle and inconspicuous with his approach.

Now...there are women who take advantage of the friend zone and use it for their convenience. It can become a safety net in which women put guys into a category of "I will never ever sleep with him but I don't want to be mean so I'll just keep him around because he's nice and feeds me emotionally". Women also send mixed messages to guys they aren't interested in because they like attention; so she constantly flirts and leads him on knowing that she has no real intention on sleeping with him. *This is dangerous!* No guy just wants to be friends with you if he approaches you, flirts with you, asks you out to dinner, or exhibits any other behavior that shows his interest. If you are not interested in him beyond a platonic friendship then you need to let him know and not make him guess. When you put a guy in the friend zone without letting him know that you are only interested in him as a friend you are stringing him along. And I don't think you'd like anyone doing that to you!

There are some of us who do have guy friends and are comfortable with those relationships. With that, I've heard that there's no way that men and women can form platonic relationships – I both agree and disagree. I have guy friends who I would never cross the line with, and a guy friend or two who I have already crossed the line with but decided not to anymore, because I value their friendship, their opinion, and what they stand for and don't want sex to cloud or confuse the relationship. This doesn't mean that they aren't attracted to me or that I'm not attracted to them but drawing that boundary is necessary for me. By drawing a line they can then decide whether or not they'd like to continue with a platonic friendship or if they'd like to pursue their interests in a separate direction. Looking for a guy to be upfront with you about what he wants when he approaches you is unnecessary because what he wants is already encoded in the fact that he even approached you. Again, this doesn't mean that he isn't looking for a serious relationship or that he doesn't want to have an emotional connection; but just know that he absolutely wants sex as well. If you aren't willing to go there with him then don't string him along. Learn how to be polite but honest so that there is no ambiguity in you turning him down. If you start getting to know him but realize that you aren't interested in having sex with him, you should let him know that you aren't interested in moving the relationship forward.

A guy will want to have sex with every woman that he approaches. A lady won't want to have sex with every guy that approaches her. The rule of thumb is for us to be honest about how we feel without having to throw a jab at his ego. We know what he wants already and if we aren't willing to give it to him then we shouldn't entertain the conversation. No more putting guys in the friend zone – speak up and open your mind, you know, before you open your legs!